'Climb the mountains and get their good tidings. Nature's peace will flow into you as sunshine flows into trees. The winds will blow their own freshness into you, and the storms their energy, while cares will drop away from you like the leaves of autumn.'

John Muir, *The Mountains of California*

Creative team

Contributors

Images

Editor-in-chief
Carole Bamford

Creative Director
Claudie Dubost

Editorial Director
Imogen Fortes

Contributing Editor
Sophie Richardson

Editorial Assistant
Lisa Perry

Production Coordinator
Matthew Gorman

Digital Content Editor
Rose Slavin

Printed in the United
Kingdom at
Sherwin Rivers Ltd
on 100% recycled paper
using vegetable inks.

Cover photography by
Richard Gaston

@seed_magazine

Words
Carole Bamford
Leonora Bamford
Alice B-B
Emma Crichton-Miller
Catherine Early
Jo Fairley
Imogen Fortes
Lisa Grainger
Phoebe Hunt
Satish Kumar
Fiona McCarthy
Ben Olsen
Sophie Richardson
Jez Taylor

Recipes
Gaven Fuller
Dominique Park

Photography
Alex Baxter
Kasia Bobula
Charlie Burrell
Samuel Churchill
Sylvain Deleu
Richard Gaston
Matthew Gorman
Misan Harriman
Giada Mariani
Eckhart Matthäus
Lizzie Mayson
Gilbert McCarragher
Martin Morrell
Matt Palmer
Carolyn Quartermaine
Gerrit Schreurs
Jacob van der Beugel
Sarah Weal
Marco Zanta

Styling
Claudie Dubost
Frankie Unsworth

Illustration
Marc Majewski
Blandine Pannequin

Contents

06
in conversation with Misan Harriman
The photographer and founder of *What We Seee*, who made history as the first black person to shoot the cover of British *Vogue*'s September issue, discusses the power of the photographic image and its ability to motivate change

14
wilder farming and rewilding
The rewilding movement is gaining in popularity, but not everyone is convinced of its benefits – we look at examples around the UK to consider both sides of the argument

22
embracing the stillness
The architect John Pawson reflects on his career of minimalist design and contemplates whether living in a considered, calm space can make us feel more at peace

32
conscious cloth
The Sustainable Angle's founder Nina Marenzi outlines why the fashion industry needs to rethink the materials it uses and turn to regenerative forms of agriculture to lighten its environmental footprint and even help repair some of the damage it has caused

34
the essence of the past
Jo Fairley, co-founder of The Perfume Society, meets the perfumer Lyn Harris to discuss how fragrance is entwined with memory and why it has the ability to affect our mood and wellbeing

38
crossed pathways
The artist inspired by science, Jacob van der Beugel, discusses his bold installations, which invite us to consider how our future is linked to our biology, and the memory and legacy of our past

46
read the (carbon) label
As consumers become more environmentally conscious, the enterprise Carbon Calories plans to make choices easier by providing carbon emission data

50
eat well
A selection of seasonal recipes reflecting our belief that to eat well is to eat locally, in season, organically and without waste

68
roots entwined
Jenny Crisp has woven baskets by hand for 35 years. By tending and growing her own willow the artisan has an instinctive understanding of her material, which informs her designs

76
mead
We investigate why the honey-based drink is being revived around the world, delighting local beekeepers

82
travel is precious
The travel landscape has been shaken beyond recognition but Alice B-B hopes that the Covid-19 pandemic will inspire a new kind of travel, driven by opportunities to make a positive impact

84
call of the wild
We visit the Scottish estate, Wildland, which is proving to be a haven for wildlife and guests alike

92
winter planting
The head of Daylesford farm's market garden Jez Taylor discusses what vegetables you can look to plant and grow through the colder months

94
garden crafts
How to make block prints sourced from the soil and other creative activities inspired by the great outdoors

98
a table for autumn
A gathering of foraged finds and colours to inspire a seasonal table setting

102
a command from nature
The Covid-19 pandemic has caused much suffering but for many lockdown was an intervention, forcing us to pause and reflect. Satish Kumar considers whether we can hope to see lasting change after the crisis

Seed likes

A BOOK

'A Monk's Guide to Happiness'
by Gelong Thubten

A PLACE

Bantham Beach
Devon, England

A POEM

'An English Breeze'
Robert Louis Stevenson

A TABLE

The Hidden Hut
Portscatho, Cornwall, England

AN EXHIBITION

Paradise Lost
at Kew Gardens, London

Editor's letter

PORTRAIT Martin Morrell

As the end of a year that has brought hardship and challenge draws near, our third volume of *Seed* looks to the future: to how we can grow and build on our experiences, as well as draw hope in a time of turmoil.

With our worlds upended, we sought to balance the confinement of lives led indoors with time spent outdoors. We found refuge in nature's open spaces and calm through its constant, steadying presence. This issue is a celebration of that sanctuary.

Our writers travel to Scotland to explore the wilds of the Scottish Highlands and discover how our journeys can be a force for change when conservation and tourism unite with sensitivity. We share the stories of the artists and craftspeople who find not only beauty and meaning in nature, but harvest its gifts to make their living and create their work. And we consider whether this period of slower living has cultivated the awareness to drive a shift in our behaviour and patterns of consumption that the planet so plainly needs.

The world may remain unpredictable for a while longer, and we are left with the sense that life feels more fragile than it once did. But what is evidenced by this time of reflection is the strength in our ability to bring about change when we adopt a community mindset and act together. Can we sustain this awakening and set ourselves on a different course? My hope is that we can.

– Carole Bamford

IN CONVERSATION WITH
MISAN HARRIMAN

WORDS Carole Bamford
PHOTOGRAPHY Samuel Churchill (portrait), Misan Harriman

Misan Harriman is a photographer, creative director and cultural curator. He is the founder of *What We Seee*, a digital media platform whose mission is to democratise access to music, film, art and culture; to act as a digital custodian, curating and amplifying a diverse and eclectic array of voices and artists in order to raise the tone of cultural conversation on the internet. Born in Nigeria but raised in England, Harriman recently became the first black person in Vogue's 104-year history to shoot the cover of its September issue. But it is his arresting, emotive and powerful imagery documenting the Black Lives Matter movement in London this summer that has captured a mood and a moment in history, and reveals the power an image holds, with its ability to embolden, inspire and galvanise a nation.

You are a self-taught photographer, which is both exceptional and unusual. You changed your career significantly to pursue photography; what is it that drew you to the medium?

Throughout my whole life I've been obsessed with music, film and photography. The still and moving image have always been my escape, so although I recently picked up a camera, I would say that my love affair with imagery has existed since my eyes opened. I was the guy that always annoyed my friends by talking about the great photojournalists of different eras, or by banging on about Cecil Beaton, Norman Parkinson, Irving Penn, Sally Mann, Gordon Parks and Charlie Phillips. The idea of these men and women who could take a camera and show us the meaning of life in some small way struck me as very romantic. And that's what I think the power of photography is; it isn't just freezing a moment – it's letting us understand what that moment was. I suppose that because I had worshipped these people for most of my life, I was very intimidated to even attempt to pick up a camera or be an image-maker myself. And although I haven't had any formal training, I've been training my eye from birth, which is possibly why I've jumped quite far in terms of where I've got to with the camera. The tool was looking for me and we finally found each other.

Edward Enninful (editor-in-chief of British *Vogue*) has described your work as 'era-defining'. What is it that you think he sees or feels in your images that defines this time?

Edward is in a category of genius which means that many of us don't see the world through his lens. This man was just on the cover of *Time* magazine for good reason. He didn't need anyone to tell him what he knew I had. He saw in me what, frankly, I didn't see in myself. Not only does he recognise talent, he recognises the right moment for somebody's story to be told. He knows how to communicate that person's story and he also knows how to empower them to ensure they have wings once it has been released into the world. I'm forever grateful to have had this man guide me in the way that he has, because I've struggled my whole life with imposter syndrome and self-doubt, and to have somebody who has seen it all tell you that you're more than good enough, is remarkable.

Why do you choose to photograph in black and white?

I love the relationship between light and shadows, and the tonality of monochrome. I think it cuts away so much of the noise in telling the story of an image, and it leads the eye to really take in the photograph. Don't

get me wrong, colour photography – with all the spectrums of colour that the human eye can see – is also incredible but I found that some of the most moving images, if you look at the 100 most important pictures ever taken, will be in black and white. And there's something about black and white – especially with civil rights photography – that just conjures up the purpose of power in a way that I haven't been able to witness in colour.

Great photography is great photography, but somehow to me black and white photography feels a little bit more powerful.

What would you tell a young person today who was worried about starting out in the industry?

The internet breaks down a lot of the social and economic barriers that have been there in the past. Now, if you put your work out there people will respond. I had no idea that people would react to my civil rights imagery in the way that they did – I just put the images on Instagram. At that point I didn't have many followers but the conversations about the photographs and their reach just kicked off – massively.

Your editorial philosophy for *What We Seee* is that whatever you publish has to make people feel, learn or think

something – that culture is not just there to distract or entertain. You've talked about the notion of 'cultural nutrition' – what is it that you're hoping to feed people through cultural diversity and through the platform?

What We Seee is a digital platform, a publishing house really, that is for all those who are drowning in the noise of the internet. We are this curated life raft that is saving you from viral fodder, and giving you your digital five-a-day.

If you listen to 'Harvest Moon' by Neil Young, you don't need anyone to tell you what an extraordinary piece of music it is, and that is my prime understanding of art. It is the only thing I've come across that as mankind we cannot defend ourselves against. Whether it's listening to Maria Callas, Nina Simone or Bob Marley, it seeps into your bones. And what I do is use that to help people see the very best of the human condition, to help people understand who they are and where they're headed. I do that with writing, with film, with music – with any creative art form. I find the best of it and I share it with as many people as possible. And I've been able to do it at scale – we reach well over a billion people a year.

People have the hunger for it, especially now. The age of people consuming rubbish that is not good

for their mental health is finally
beginning to end. And people are
really beginning to understand that
what they put into their minds, just
like what they put into their bodies
through their food, can be detrimental
to their wellbeing. And if I can curate
and help you manage your digital diet,
then I'll be a happy man.

And yet while a lot of the content on
What We Seee **is there to uplift and
inspire, a diversity of content means
that there are, of course, stories that
are not so joyful, because they tell
truths, and these might provoke
anxiety or a different kind of reaction
in their reader or viewer and might
be deemed to have a 'negative' impact
on someone's mental health. Do you
think the responsibility for choosing
consumption lies with the individual
or with you as the curator?**

I want you to learn, laugh and cry.
All three are really important to your
mental health.

I was talking recently about crying
and how good it is to let your soul leak.
I think there are many stories that
we publish that are very, very moving
– and will have you in pieces. But
what we won't do is publish misogyny,
racism and stuff that may get a lot
of attention but that simply isn't good
for you. If we move you to tears then
so be it.

As you mentioned, you've been open on your own social media platform about experiencing self-doubt and suffering from imposter syndrome. I wondered whether you think there is a power in sharing feelings online?

I've always thought it's important and I think that now it's more important than ever. The biggest mental health epidemic is upon us following the pandemic, and for many people of a diverse background that's coupled with the largest civil rights movement of all time – that is a lot to unpack. If I can use culture to help people handle the onshore waters that we're all trying to navigate, then for me it's more than a duty; it's something I really believe will help people steady their sails.

My own mental health has been very much helped by the access – through privilege, frankly speaking – to the very best in arts and culture and I want to democratise that and give it to anyone with two things: an inquisitive mind and an internet connection.

Seed's philosophy is to advocate living a more sustainable and conscious way of life – in large part by coming back to nature and connecting with it as best we can. What has been your own experience of nature and your relationship with it, and is it something you feel is important for our mental health?

Massively. Three years ago, I got what I call my 'firstborn' – my dog. He's a Hungarian vizsla called Nelson. I live in the countryside and I am fortunate to have access to relatively raw nature within the Surrey Hills. There is no event or party that could ever mean as much to me as my 7am walks with Nelson and my moment of solitude with him. Walking with an animal makes me connect to the outdoors in a way that me just going on a walk wouldn't – as much as I enjoy going on walks. Watching him take in and look at the world through a completely different lens to mine reminds me to respect the natural world.

There's a great quote by the playright William Inge, which states that we 'have treated our distant cousins in fur and feathers so badly that beyond doubt, if they were able to formulate a religion, they would depict the devil in human form', and I love that quote because it reminds me how incredibly selfish mankind has been with regard to what we're doing with global warming, and just generally how so many species have been eradicated. And it's only increasing at a pace that is very hard to comprehend.

I love the idea of a more sustainable existence, ranging from our mental health to the way we live our lives and raise our families, through to understanding that the trees that look down on us have been there much longer than we have and we should stop embarrassing ourselves in front of them.

Do you think the arts can help to progress the fight against climate change?

Yes, of course. I publish a lot of quotes and poetry that talk about how important the natural world has always been. And sometimes reading a really moving poem or hearing a certain piece of music makes you remember that it's not just about us.

Over the past year we've seen a lot of imagery related to the environment and the devastation we're causing. Do you think we've become numb to imagery like the fires in California or the Amazon's deforestation?

It depends how much empathy you have in your heart. I say this repeatedly, but you're not born with a finite amount of empathy in you. So many humans guard how much empathy they give, reserving it for their family and friends. If you feed it, it grows – almost like a plant within you. If you look at certain world leaders who are devoid of empathy it's because they were never fed it. So, when you look at the fires and the colour of the skies, I don't know how that can't move you or can't make you think, 'this is a warning'.

And if anything, this moment of lockdown should have been a reset – a chance for all of us to think about how we are going to look after ourselves and Mother Earth. It is extraordinary that in 2020 we're living through earthquakes, hurricanes, forest fires, a global pandemic, plagues – and that they're hitting us all at once. To me that must make us take stock and reflect on what we can do to improve how we're treating Mother Earth – she's clearly not happy or healthy – and she's the only mother we have so we need to look after her.

What is on the horizon for you and for *What We Seee*?

To continue to reach the hearts and minds of people. *What We Seee* and myself are intrinsically linked, so I want to keep growing the business, to keep making beautiful formats, to keep empowering and shining a light on – hopefully young – people that deserve a voice and have never had an opportunity. For my side, I'm getting into film-making, so my hope is for my lens to find stories that are worth telling and that people will like the way that I tell them. And to be a somewhat present father and husband.

WILDER FARMING AND REWILDING –

THE FUTURE FOR OUR LANDSCAPES?

WORDS Catherine Early
PHOTOGRAPHY Charlie Burrell

Rewilding is going mainstream, with new projects popping up and a surge in demand for information. But it will need to overcome misconceptions of its aims to succeed.

In a year overshadowed by the Covid-19 pandemic, flooding and extreme heat, people have been desperate for positive stories. Much of these have come from wildlife – white storks have bred in the wild in the UK for the first time in over 600 years, bison are headed for a comeback in Kent and reintroduced beavers have finally been approved by the government.

These successes are all part of the same movement – rewilding. An idea that has leapt from obscurity to mainstream in just a few years, rewilding is defined by its proponents as large-scale restoration of ecosystems using natural processes, where nature can look after itself. It can also involve the reintroduction of species that had previously been driven out.

Rewilding is fundamentally different to traditional conservation approaches, which tend to be driven by specific goals or target specific species. 'Such strategies are not working in terms of preserving biodiversity as a whole, or getting ecosystems to function properly,' says author and conservationist Isabella

Tree, whose book *Wilding: The Return of Nature to a British Farm* tells the story of the now famous rewilding project at Knepp Farm, West Sussex, where she lives with her husband Charlie Burrell.

'[That's] not to knock conventional conservation projects,' she adds, 'because without them, many species would have become extinct. But these areas are Noah's arks – if they are not bigger and connected and fully functioning, those little islands are doomed to fail. Wildlife needs connected areas so that it can move between them and expand populations. If a species has been helped in an area but can't expand, the population can only increase so far. Even with everything we've thrown at it, biodiversity in the UK is still crashing.'

The 3,500-acre Knepp estate was once intensively farmed. In 2001, its owners, Tree and Burrell, began a pioneering rewilding project, driving habitat creation using grazing animals and the restoration of natural water courses. Over the years, an increasing number of very rare species have come to breed

on the land, including turtle doves, nightingales, peregrine falcons and purple emperor butterflies.

As a pioneering project, Knepp initially encountered resistance from neighbouring landowners who thought the land looked 'messy', and was also caught up in lengthy government bureaucracy and feasibility studies. However, it is now heralded as the inspiration for a much bigger movement that has gained ground at a pace Tree describes as 'astonishing'.

'It's really in the past two to three years that we've seen a dramatic change in people's outlook and imagination. Rewilding has reached popular perception, rather than being something that just ecologists talk about,' she says.

As well as benefitting wildlife and plants, rewilding ecosystems can transform the land's ability to soak up carbon emissions. Rewilding Britain, an organisation which formed in 2015 to advocate for the idea and support those who are planning rewilding projects, estimates that six

million hectares of restored peatbogs, woodland, heaths and grassland could absorb more than 10 per cent of current UK greenhouse gas emissions. Local communities can also benefit from the projects, with jobs created in wildlife tourism and hospitality.

Rewilding projects have sprung up all over the UK. Wild Ennerdale in the Lake District is reducing the numbers of grazing sheep on its land, adding small numbers of horses and cattle instead as it believes these have less impact on the soil and are beneficial for the transport of seeds. The project will enable natural regeneration which is much better for biodiversity, cost and carbon sequestration than planting trees. They are also 'rewilding' the river – allowing it to spread and spill and have its way, which is having flood mitigation effects downstream.

Trees for Life's Dundreggan rewilding estate in the heart of the Scottish Highlands has seen the first breeding pair of golden eagles on the site in

40 years and is planning to open a public rewilding centre in 2022.

One of the newest rewilding projects, Wild East, launched in July, aims to bring landowners and the public together to turn 250,000 hectares of land in East Anglia over to nature by 2070.

'A year or so ago, we were going to farmers and landowners to talk about rewilding, now they're coming to us,' says a spokesperson for Rewilding Britain. 'In the past 12 months, we've spoken to over 50 landowners and partnerships, who are managing some 200,000 acres of land between them,' he adds.

However, the rewilding movement has been hampered by misunderstandings about its aims. A key example of this is the Sea to Summit project in Wales, which covers the area from the Pumlumon massif in mid-Wales to the Dyfi estuary and Cardigan Bay. Encompassing several

biodiversity-rich areas, such as the UNESCO-designated Dyfi Biosphere reserve, the project aims to improve connectivity between these landscapes to benefit nature, for example by giving wildlife space to move between them.

The project, which had £3.4 million of funding, was looking for landowners and farmers to come forward and take part in schemes to restore and expand habitats, such as blanket bog, grasslands and saltmarsh, in ways that would benefit native wildlife, including pine martens and horseshoe bats, while also creating jobs for local people.

However, in October 2019 Rewilding Britain pulled out of the project, citing opposition from farmers' unions and some local people. 'There'd been stories in the local press about the project, which we kept saying weren't the case – we weren't reintroducing bears and wolves, and we weren't forcing farmers off land, that's not how we work,' the

spokesperson for Rewilding Britain says. 'In the end, we decided that our presence wasn't helping, so we withdrew to allow for more positive constructive communication with farmers, councillors and communities to take place,' he explains.

RSPB Cymru has now taken over management of the project, and is undertaking further consultation with local communities. Elwyn Vaughan, a Plaid Cymru councillor for Powys Council, and chair of community group Copa (Cymunedau Oll Pumlumon a'r Ardal), which opposed Rewilding Britain's plans, says that local people had felt a lack of community ownership under Rewilding Britain's plans. The new consultations with RSPB Cymru were far more positive, he believes.

'The farmers would argue that they already do a lot of nature-based farming; if someone comes from outside and forces another layer on it, that's antagonising.

But if they are seen as central to it, they feel a sense of ownership,' says Vaughan.

He points to a separate project to reintroduce pine martens led by the Vincent Wildlife Trust as the model Copa would like others to follow. 'The people behind that went out of their way to talk to farmers and landowners to ascertain that they were happy for pine martens to be part of the local ecosystem,' he says.

An organisation for local landowners in Penrith in the Lake District has sought advice from the group, Vaughan reports. 'They have similar concerns about a rewilding initiative there. This seems to be a common issue – you want to avoid the perception of middle-class do-gooders coming to the area and telling the locals what to do. That is the kiss of death for any project.'

In June this year, non-executive director of the Department for Environment, Food and Rural Affairs (Defra) Ben Goldsmith suggested that rewilding should be renamed 'wilder farming' in order to reassure farmers that they are central to the movement.

Writing in industry magazine *Farmers Guardian*, he argued that the media had created the idea that rewilding was the preserve of 'trendy metropolitan eco-zealots' who wanted to 'drive out traditional farming', but claimed this was not the case. Vaughan agrees, saying the term 'rewilding' should be 'thrown out of the window'.

'It creates antagonism: to some it means going back to nature, but to others it means the introduction of wolves and bears.'

Isabella Tree agrees: 'I think Ben has a really good point. The media loves polarising rewilding and farming, but it's not helpful or appropriate. Rewilding itself is never going to be about maximising production of food – like farming is – though you can produce meat from the free-roaming animals that are used to drive habitat recovery for rewilding. Rewilding is about restoring biodiversity and the natural processes that support a sustainable environment. But farming has to work with natural processes, too – it has to get "wilder", in Ben's terms. We have to stop ploughing and using chemicals – or we'll lose our soil as every civilisation in history has done before us. Farming has to become "regenerative" and there are farmers all over the globe, now, from Gabe Brown in the States, to Charlie Massy in Australia who are showing how we can do this: proving that it is not only sustainable, it produces as much food as conventional farming and sequesters (rather than emits) carbon,' explains Tree. She continues: 'This is the future of farming. Rewilding is what we do with all the land in between – the marginal, inaccessible or ecologically important land. The two work hand in hand, and the ecosystem services that rewilding provides – flood prevention, soil restoration, water storage, pollinating insects and natural pest control – will, inevitably, protect our farmland and increase crop yields.

'If we can reframe farming within that ethos, with just everything getting wilder, and working with natural processes rather than battling against them all the time, that's the same page that we have to be on,' she says.

Rewilding Britain believes that restoring nature on a large scale can be achieved without loss of productive farmland. 'There's huge areas where we can do a lot more, such as areas of poorly-managed peatland, grouse moors, large spaces in Scotland which should really be native forest,' the spokesperson says.

When Tree and Burrell embarked on the Knepp project, they set up an advisory board to help them, which Tree says was 'incredibly useful'. A team of scientists and ecologists not only gave technical support on particular issues, but also gave the project credibility. She recommends this approach for anyone undertaking rewilding. 'They don't have powers as such, they're just knowledgeable, like-minded people who are excited about the project. It's wonderful for morale – there will be good and bad times,' she says.

Much effort is going into technical support for rewilding. Knepp itself runs practical workshops for landowners and conservation organisations. Later this year, Rewilding Britain is to launch a network to 'spearhead rapid and massively upscaled rewilding', bringing together landowners, farmers, land managers, community groups and local authorities across Britain, who are rewilding land or considering doing so. Its initial aim is to catalyse and support the rewilding of at least 300,000 acres – an area the size of the North York Moors National Park – within three years. 'While the enthusiasm is there, the knowledge and expertise of how to rewild often isn't, so the network has increasingly made sense,' the Rewilding Britain spokesperson says.

Tree believes that the more people who are involved the better. 'Rewilding is not just something for the specialised few with 1,000 acres – it's for everyone's back garden, roadside verge, cemetery, allotments, tow paths or railway embankments. Everything can be managed in a much wilder way, and I think that really involves us all.'

www.knepp.co.uk
www.rspb.org.uk

EMBRACING THE STILLNESS

WORDS Sophie Richardson
PHOTOGRAPHY Gilbert McCarragher,
Eckhart Matthäus, Marco Zanta

One of the most influential architects of his generation, John Pawson is known for his slow, considered designs that are as much about a way of life as they are refined aesthetics. Here, he looks back on a career that has redefined minimalism and considers whether a calm interior can lead to a calmer state of mind.

When John Pawson first envisaged building a family country retreat, he couldn't possibly have foreseen what a literal place of refuge it would become.

Completed towards the end of last year, Home Farm was the realisation of a long-held dream to create a place for Pawson and his wife, Catherine, to escape a busy working life in London. But over the last few months the house, set deep within the Oxfordshire hills, has taken on new significance and purpose; providing a safe haven during the Covid-19 pandemic, as well as a calming antidote to the drama and anxiety that unfurled outside.

Made up of a cluster of agricultural buildings dating from the seventeenth through to the twentieth century, the Cotswold farmhouse seems like a surprising dwelling for a man dubbed the 'king of minimalism'. However, the traditional frontage masks an unexpected interior, where every aspect has been passed through an exacting filter and then further considered, refined and reduced. When we speak on the phone towards the end of lockdown, it is almost a year since completion and, if anything, the intense period of residency has proved to Pawson 'quite how deeply I love being in our home'.

The St Moritz church in Ausberg © Gilbert McCarragher

Home farm © Gilbert McCarragher

Old and new happily co-exist, with restored timber beams and door frames providing a solid framework for unapologetically contemporary features – white marble countertops, poured concrete floors and raw stainless-steel window frames containing single panes of glass that offer uninterrupted vistas of the Evenlode valley below.

There is little else to detract from the views, with superfluous details – accessories, books, general *stuff* – removed in favour of an all-enveloping simplicity. It is signature 'John Pawson'; a pared back aesthetic that has made him one of the most influential designers of his generation.

Awarded a CBE in 2019 for his services to architecture, Pawson's 40-year career has covered everything from airport lounges and hotels, to humble textiles and utility objects for the home.

Private houses make up the core of his work, but it is his sacred spaces that are particularly poignant; from the cool cloisters of the Abbey of our Lady of Nový Dvůr in Bohemia and the soaring, vaulted ceilings of the St Moritz church in Ausberg, to the quiet solitude of the Wooden Chapel in Dillingen, Germany; an intimate cabin conceived to offer shelter for passing cyclists, as well as a place to pause and reflect.

There have also been a handful of significant public commissions including the landmark 1990's Calvin Klein store on New York's Madison Avenue and, more recently, the Design Museum in London – surely the ultimate accolade for a British designer working today.

What binds them all together is Pawson's unflinching commitment to minimalism – an ethos that has defined his work since the early 1980s and can be applied to everything that he designs: from small, everyday objects such as saucepans, bowls and lights to vast architectural projects that explore fundamental principles of light, space, proportion and material.

'Simple stuff has just always appealed to me,' says the designer, when I ask about the roots of his less-is-more dogma. 'The Yorkshire moors, sixteenth-century Japan – certain cultures and trends of simplicity, were, I think, influencing me even before I started working as an architect.'

Born in Halifax, West Yorkshire, Pawson was raised alongside four elder sisters by Methodist parents who owned and ran a successful family textiles business. The plan was that Pawson would eventually take it on, but first he wished to see the world and so, aged 24, he packed his bags and headed east.

Inspired by a journey of enlightenment, Pawson headed to the picturesque Japanese temple of Eiheiji, where he imagined days spent meditating with the Zen Buddhist monks. The reality turned out to be less romantic and his residency lasted just four hours.

The culture of Japan, however – its architecture, its ceremonies, the cult of the samurai – proved to be more alluring and he stayed on for four years, the last spent in the studio of the great Shiro Kuramata – one of the most important Japanese designers of the twentieth century – who helped

Wooden Chapel in Dillingen, Germany. Eckhart Matthäus © Siegfried and Elfriede Denzel Foundation

inform Pawson's decision to become an architect. Three years of training at the Architectural Association in London followed before Pawson left – early, and therefore 'unqualified' – to set up his architectural practice in London.

A steady stream of small commercial and domestic projects followed, but it was the unexpected arrival of Calvin Klein at his studio in 1993 that heralded a new chapter in the designer's career.

'Meeting Calvin changed my life,' says Pawson today. 'And I mean literally. It changed my career and was a stepping stone to everything that has happened since.'

It wasn't just the public platform and sense of endorsement that the fashion designer offered; it was also a lesson in perfectionism. 'His influence,' says Pawson, 'was huge.'

'Everything Calvin did and everything he touched, whether it was the advertising, the branding, the scent, the clothes or the stores, he did at the very highest level. I was already interested in exploring how I could do things "the best". But with Calvin, you learnt so much about editing and about dealing with people and personalities. It was fascinating.'

When the Calvin Klein flagship store opened on Madison Avenue in 1995 it was groundbreaking in its minimalism and marked a new age for retail design. Housed in a neoclassical bank, the open plan space was lit by single panes of glass that soared 10 metres high, interspersed with stark white walls and understated displays.

This reductive aesthetic caught the eye of a group of Cistercian Trappist monks – 'and you can't get any more minimal than them' – who were the next unexpected visitors to make a pilgrimage to Pawson's London studio.

'At first I thought they'd actually been to the Calvin store, and I thought 'My god, what on earth were they doing there?' laughs Pawson. 'But I think they had actually just seen photographs of the store. And what they'd seen was a room with a couple of tables – which could well have been altars – and a space and proportions that in their head could make a nice church.

'You know, they're pragmatic people and the fact that it was a clothes shop in no way put them off. They were just after getting what they needed.'

The resulting commission was for the Abbey of our Lady of Nový Dvůr in Bohemia, a project that began as a cluster of dilapidated agricultural buildings arranged around a courtyard and which, over a number of years, has been transformed into an elegant cloister complex encompassing an abbey, guest houses, workshop and freestanding chapel. For Pawson it remains 'the project of a lifetime'.

The leap from Madison Avenue to monastery did not in any way faze Pawson, and he applies the same principles and vision for all of his designs: 'I want people to feel at home in everything I make, whether it's a store or an airport lounge – even on a bridge,' says the designer, adding that he wants people to feel 'quietly exhilarated, but most of all comfortable – both physically and mentally'.

'There is no architecture without light.'

current average CO₂ emissions for a dwelling.

'Sustainability is now at the heart of everything that we do as architects, and I think my clients always tend to want to push things further,' says Pawson. 'They're more "green" and they're more sustainable than the regulations. And that keeps things very interesting.'

For all his projects he strives to use natural materials – 'surfaces that please the eye and feel good to the touch' – and wherever possible he likes to work with local stone or timber, not only for their environmental benefits but also to 'embed a piece of architecture in its site, visually and emotionally.'

Above all else, however, it is natural light that is at the heart of Pawson's designs; indeed, he would argue, it is at the heart of all architecture itself. 'There is no architecture without light,' he says. 'I mean that obviously material

and proportion and scale and mass and all of the other elements form architecture or form structure. But for me, light is probably the single most important element of all my work.'

Watching the changes in light slowly unfold around him has been one of the unexpected pleasures of the last few months at Home Farm, and if anything, his appreciation for the slow principles that have underpinned his career – and his home – have amplified during this time of repose.

'I've always enjoyed being out in landscape, but the current circumstances have brought a different intensity to the experience,' says Pawson. 'Lockdown has made me realise how much of my energy is normally consumed by either constantly thinking about or making the next journey. It's oddly liberating to have these choices temporarily removed and to immerse yourself in where you are: to embrace the stillness.'

Nina Marenzi is the founder of The Sustainable Angle, a not-for-profit organisation that initiates and supports projects with a focus on sustainability in the fashion and textile industries, as well as related industries, such as food and agriculture. Each year the organisation hosts the Future Fabrics Expo in London, which has become the largest dedicated showcase of innovative and sustainable materials for the fashion industry. The Sustainable Angle's aim is to act as a vehicle for change – to help drive the industry towards having a positive impact on nature and communities by working with sustainably-produced textiles that are safe, renewable, restorative and apply responsible practices throughout their supply chain. We spoke to Marenzi about why the fashion industry needs to 'diversify its fibre basket', how what we wear affects the health of the planet's soil, and how fashion can help to be part of the environmental solution rather than the problem.

WORDS Imogen Fortes

CONSCIOUS CLOTH
THE FUTURE OF FASHION AND ITS FABRICS

Where does your interest in nature and your desire to support it stem from?

I grew up in Switzerland, outside of Zurich not too far from the mountains, and contact with nature was just part of our existence. One of my earliest memories is walking home from school with a friend playing with snails – we would pick them off trees to observe them close up. I used to help my mother in the garden, planting and growing tomatoes, and that scent and the feeling of plucking tomatoes still warm from the sun is still very vivid. It was always just clear to me that you were part of nature and you needed to look after it and respect it.

The environment has always been a big thing in my life; I started by working in environmental policy, and one of my first jobs was volunteering at Greenpeace where I manned the phones taking questions from the public. I studied political science and did several Masters degrees – the last one was on sustainable agriculture and rural development, which is all about the importance of soil.

Why is soil so important for the fashion supply chain?

Fashion is dependent on its raw materials, and unless these are synthetic, most of them are natural fibres that come from or depend on the soil. We're as reliant on soil for our clothes as we are for our food.

You often speak about the need for the fashion industry to 'diversify its fibre basket' – what does that mean and why is it so important?

Again, it all comes down to the soil. We've damaged our soil to the point where we have very few growing cycles left and the fashion industry is heavily responsible for that. The industry therefore has the potential to help look after the world's soil and return it to health, or it can harm it and intensify the damage we are causing our environment.

We have to stop polluting our soil and mining its fertility because when that happens the soil can't maintain itself and the top soil becomes so dry that it gets blown off, runs into waterways and we

lose it completely. That means that future generations will no longer be able to grow anything: neither for clothing nor food. It takes about 500–1,000 years for top soil to form another 3cm.

Diversifying the fibre basket is about ensuring we widen the base of fibres we rely on to relieve the stress on the soil, and shift to textiles that are kinder to the environment. Conventional cotton and virgin polyester are currently used in over 75 per cent of all clothing created and we urgently need to move away from them. Conventional cotton is an irrigated crop so it uses a lot of water, pesticides and synthetic fertilisers, which are very polluting. Producing cotton this way is simply unsustainable for the environment and for the health of the growers and workers. And polyester is derived from petroleum, so it uses fossil fuels, which is another finite resource. Its fibres stay in the environment for hundreds of years and also contribute to the microfibre pollution in the ocean for millions of years. Anything that is not hard on the soil is an important alternative to cotton. Other natural fibres, such as hemp or linen, are inherently more sustainable.

They are hardy crops grown on marginal land, i.e. land that cannot be used for food production (unlike cotton), and they need no pesticides or synthetic fertilisers to grow. And then there's a whole range of innovative new fabrics made from agricultural waste, mushroom roots or recycled materials, which are what we showcase at the Future Fabrics Expo.

What about organic cotton – there seems to be some debate over whether that is a viable alternative and something we should or should not be using?

Organic cotton is a very different proposition to conventionally-produced cotton. Anything organic is grown in rotation, which means that you replenish the soil's nutrients with the crop that comes behind it. Growing organic cotton can have a very positive impact on soil health, especially if grown in a regenerative system, by increasing its fertility and supporting biodiversity, and healthy soil can also act as a carbon sink, capturing carbon from the atmosphere and storing it.

It's true that cotton is a very thirsty crop, but organic cotton is mainly rain-fed – globally about 80 per cent is not irrigated. The other point is that there are about 100 million people involved in cotton farming, so the social consequences of doing away with it completely would be enormously damaging, crippling the livelihoods of these people. Organic cotton is often an important cash crop that helps subsistence farmers earn the hard cash they need to buy tools or shoes for their children to be able to walk to school. For me, it's about how we grow cotton and then produce the fabric in a sustainable way to help keep those people in business.

Making visible efforts to be sustainable is something that every fashion brand now has to consider, but when you launched The Sustainable Angle in 2010 the landscape must have been very different. How was your work received then?

In the last 18 months things have changed a lot – we'd reached a tipping point just before Covid-19. When we launched, nobody wanted to talk about sustainable fabrics; designers really had to be convinced by alternatives and sustainability had to be 'demystified'. But creative people do look for new things and once they were shown the fabrics they were 'converted'. Touch plays a significant part in this process. And ultimately, no designer wants to create polluting fashion, so they were inspired by the potential for change and also for experimentation.

And our role has also evolved. At the beginning The Sustainable Angle was largely about making it easy for people to access these new materials, and breaking the stigma around the likes of hemp or jute, which were not considered appealing or viable alternatives, by showing them as part of sophisticated blends. Now, we're more like policemen – there is so much greenwashing in textiles and fashion that we're doing a lot of research and sharing this information: checking suppliers' background and claims and providing education and labelling around what's truly more sustainable. Our focus is on making it easy for fashion brands and designers to find more sustainable materials.

Besides the fibres and fabrics themselves, what are the other aspects that clothing brands need to address to be offering their customers true transparency and a guarantee they are following tangible ethical and environmental principles?

At The Sustainable Angle, we have four criteria used to assess a fabric's sustainability: water usage and the treatment of water; respect for biodiversity; what types of energy are used and how much; and how much waste was generated in producing that fabric. These are all things that a brand needs to consider in its choice of fabric, but producing clothing goes beyond that and it's crucial to consider a garment's entire lifecycle.

There are potentially a lot of chemicals involved in the garment's creation and processing: in dyes; the water treatment; how the fibre is treated with finishing agents; in stain-resistant applicants.

Textile chemistry has greatly evolved over the last 10 years and there are now non-toxic chemicals used by the more progressive textile mills and suppliers.

What will happen to that material at the end of the garment's life is also crucial. Often the biggest impact is in the user phase – how we look after that piece of clothing and how long we keep it really does affect its environmental footprint. Not using a tumble dryer and always hanging clothes up to dry are really important in terms of helping to conserve energy usage. As is taking care of our clothes so that they last.

And finally, certifications, such as GOTS (Global Organic Textile Standard) are important in terms of transparency as they are about meeting organic standards across the whole supply chain. That's also why you pay more for clothes that are certified as every step in this long chain is assured.

Over the course of this year, many people have re-examined their relationship with their wardrobe, perhaps wearing less or reconsidering the brands they support? Do you think this period will influence attitudes to fashion and purchasing choices henceforth?

Hugely. Certainly we've seen that lots of brands have doubled down on their commitment to act responsibly. It's not as easy right now, but of the brands we work with nobody is pulling back from their commitment. And from a customer perspective, we've seen that there is a demand from those who want to see brands behaving responsibly. During Covid-19 people have learned more about the impacts of human behaviour on the environment but this period is just a blip – the effects of the climate crisis are going to be far worse than Covid-19. The momentum we've seen needs to continue; we have to reduce our greenhouse gas emissions otherwise we are going above the global warming limit, raising the planet's temperature by 1.5°C beyond pre-industrial levels, and the consequences of this are frightening and will be felt by all of us.

THE ESSENCE OF THE PAST

WORDS Jo Fairley
PHOTOGRAPHY Giada Mariani, Kasia Bobula, Carolyn Quartermaine

Lyn Harris sat down with Jo Fairley, co-founder of The Perfume Society, in the perfumer's boutique in London's Marylebone, to discuss fragrance, its link with memory and wellbeing, and the inspirations behind the exquisite fragrances Harris blends, using some of the world's finest ingredients.

Jo Fairley: Why is it that scent triggers memories in such a vivid way?

Lyn Harris: When we smell something, it hits the limbic part of the brain, which is attached to memory – and that's why the initial 'oh, wow!' is so immediate: that's the brain channelling, 'you've smelled that before' – though it takes a while to figure out what the association is. That olfactory part of us is so complex. It's something we don't always acknowledge, but actually, we're animals. And although we don't like to talk about it (and I'm often shut up at dinner parties when I bring this up!), animals are attracted to each other by smells. That hidden subconscious olfactory element is what's so mysterious and fascinating to me.

JF: As someone who loves to smell everything around me, I'm always astonished to meet people who seem somehow 'cut off' from their sense of smell.

LH: Totally. As we grow up, we're encouraged to hide the natural smells. It's weird, but as a perfumer, I'm briefed to create fragrances to disguise those – which is so ironic, because I'm inspired by the basic smells of life.

JF: What is your own first scent memory?

LH: I spent a lot of time with my grandparents at their home in a little village between Inverness and Aberdeen. The whole experience was incredibly fragrant: my grandmother grew sweet peas and I'm obsessed with them now. My grandfather was a carpenter; I remember the smell of wood on him, the scent of the wood shavings in his workshop and even in his pockets. There isn't a day that goes by when I don't think of them.

JF: It's amazing how often people share scent memories of their grandparents, I find. My grandmother would rub my fingers on geranium leaves in her lean-to greenhouse off the kitchen, and when I do that now in my own greenhouse the memory is so vivid that I can not only see her face but the print on her dress.

©Carolyn Quartermaine

LH: It's such a gift to be able to enjoy smells like that. I honestly believe we should be talking about scents and aromas much more than we do. Ironically, Covid-19 has done a huge amount to tune people into their sense of smell, because the loss of that sense is a sign of potential infection. (I certainly know a lot of people who have lost their sense of smell, mostly temporarily, this year.) But I have faith that just as we all began to tune into food, a decade or two back, connecting with producers and artisans and learning to taste, the same is starting to happen with fragrance. At last!

JF: It's a long way from smelling wood shavings in your grandfather's shed to becoming a perfumer, though.

LH: A really important part of my journey was working at a shop called Irvine Lodge in my home town of Halifax, run by two incredibly inspiring people – he was a yoga expert who used to do yoga in front of me in the shop; she was this glamorous woman who loved having her hair done and adored fragrance. It was a complete mecca for the wealthy of the area, stocking all the great French houses like Guerlain, Chanel, Nina Ricci, as well as Estée Lauder. I started as a Saturday girl; I was terrible at school and after I was asked to leave, which mortified me at the time – I went to work there for a year. I became obsessed and studied all the great perfume houses and the fragrance families.

JF: And then you trained as an aromatherapist – before I first met you, even before you went off to train at the Cinquième Sens fragrance school in Paris.

LH: Yes, I was lucky enough to train with the founders of Aromatherapy Associates, who taught me so, so much.

They used to import astonishing essential oils; there was one particular grapefruit from Florida that would just blow my mind.

JF: Don't you wish that there was more research into how perfume can affect your mood and wellbeing, as we all know aromatherapy oils can? Because I certainly use it to uplift or ground me...

LH: Fragrance definitely has that power. My father is in a care home in Harrogate and the nurses call up and say: 'Your dad needs his fragrance; it's what's keeping him going.' That's part of its magic: perfume can cheer us up, or soothe us, exactly like aromatherapy oils can; it can connect people with their spirituality, as smoke has always done – and, of course, perfume got its name from *per fumum*, or 'through smoke'. In fact, I never go anywhere without frankincense oil on a hankie in my handbag, which I'm obsessed with. It has also been linked with spirituality for millennia and really calms me down.

JF: To me, your fragrances are different to almost anything else out there. There are so many stories woven around perfume launches, but you like to leave the raw materials to tell their own story.

LH: Yes. And I like to give them room to breathe, in a formula, by not over-complicating the list of ingredients.

I suppose if I have a signature it's a kind of simplicity. They certainly take the wearer on the journey, rather than being a wham-bam smell. What's lovely for me is to get feedback from clients – which happened so much in lockdown – about how my fragrances transported them or even 'saved' them, as they put it, at that really difficult time.

JF: I'm on a mission to help everyone really tune into and get pleasure from their sense of smell. What can people do to improve their sense of smell?

LH: I tell everyone: go out there and smell everything. Immerse yourself in perfume, get your hands on samples, go online and learn the families: the citrus, the colognes, the orientals, and start to categorise them. It's not just about smelling; it's about writing things down to 'fix' them in the brain.

JF: I get people to write everything down – what it reminds them of, a person, a place, a piece of music...

LH: Yes, just like you and geranium and your grandma. It's what perfumers do when we're learning, making associations so that we can remember all the different materials. There's a magical world of scent out there – not just in bottles, but in nature, which I think we all came to appreciate so much more this year. I just want everyone to get out there and smell it.

©Kasia Bobula, for *The New Garçonne*

©Carolyn Quartermaine

perfumerh.com
perfumesociety.org

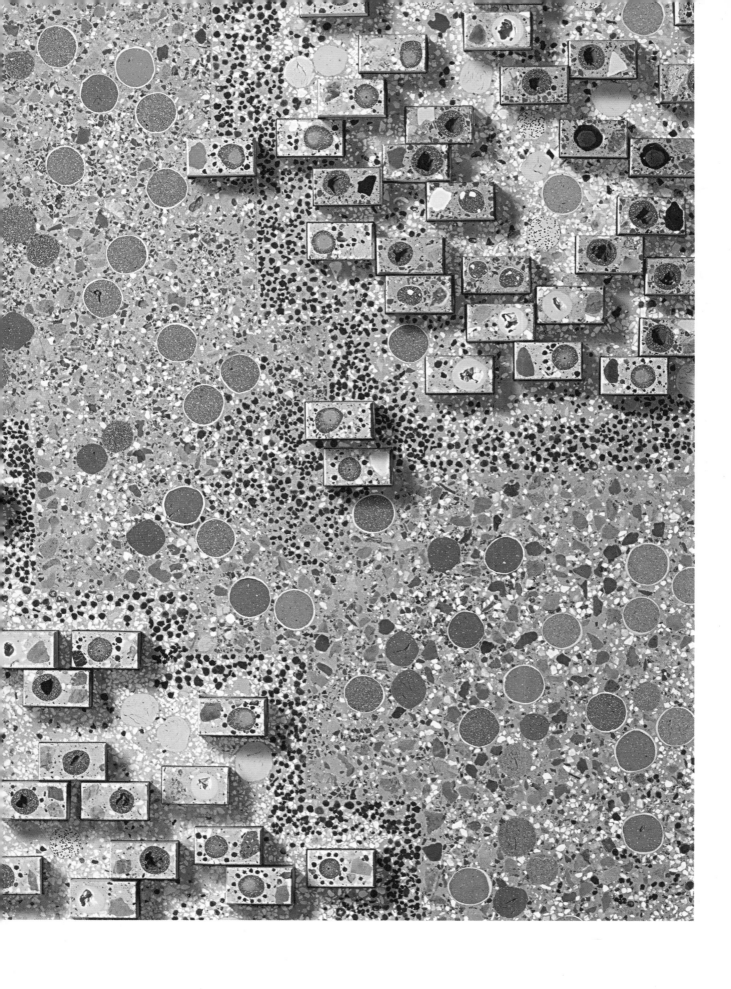

CROSSED PATHWAYS

WORDS Emma Crichton-Miller
PHOTOGRAPHY Gerrit Schreurs, Jacob van der Beugel,
Sylvain Deleu

Through the use of ceramics and cutting-edge materials
such as 'self-healing' concrete, British artist Jacob van der
Beugel creates vast abstract installations, merging art
and science to explore the human condition and question
its capacity to mutate and adapt to its future.

'A Mutating Story', detail, 2020;
Photograph: Gerrit Schreurs

Jacob van der Beugel is an ambiguous figure in the art world. He is an artist inspired by science, a humble potter who works on an ambitious scale, and who values gestural handmaking for its direct human connection while also understanding human nature through the abstract lens of DNA.

Having served his apprenticeship with two of the most renowned contemporary British potters – Edmund de Waal and Rupert Spira – he has moved on from the vessel upon which their work is based, to create abstract architectural interventions inspired by elusive scientific concepts. While he loves clay for its ancient, organic primacy, he now works regularly in concrete, that frequently abhorred modern man-made material known for its negative impact on the environment. In balancing these contradictions, van der Beugel has developed a highly

sophisticated and original hybrid practice that is partly sculpture and partly science, and which is fed by close involvement with the scientists whose cutting-edge research provides his stimulus and subject matter.

Born in the UK in 1978, van der Beugel set out to become an art historian. But while at the University of York, he started also to work with clay: 'I very much needed to work in ceramics while I was doing my degree. It brought a kind of balance,' van der Beugel explains. 'I have a propensity towards thinking when left to my own devices, which is sometimes positive and sometimes negative. I felt that clay provided an amazing grounding for articulating what I was thinking. It is so undeniably rooted to the earth that it has a universality and commonality, but also a unique ability to express human sentiments.' He adds: 'I fell in

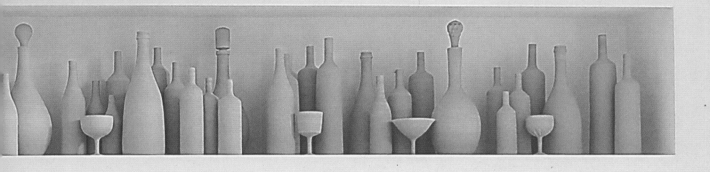

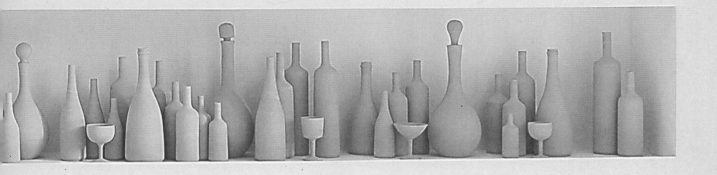

'Good Year Bad Year', 2013; Photograph: Jacob van der Beugel

love with the really traditional side of ceramics – the apprenticeships, the humility of making pots; it was very old school.' What he retained from his art history was a fascination with the tension between the grandiose notions of the Abstract Expressionist artists – 'that idea of the maker's mark, and existentialism and continual self-creation' – and the contrasting philosophy of minimalism, 'which was all about eradicating the maker's mark'.

It became apparent early on in van der Beugel's career that the vocabulary of single vessels was incompatible with what he wanted to express. He began to work in series, exploring the impact of repetition and of contrasts in form, embracing accidents and 'the way that the environment feeds into everything.' His 2013 work 'Good Year Bad Year', inspired by working vineyards, marked a culmination of this period of experimentation. Consisting of two parallel shelves of parading wine glasses and bottles, of many different forms, all unglazed, the carefully graduated differently-coloured clay bodies create a sweep of colour. It is both beautiful and philosophically charged, evoking the dimension of time: the passing of the seasons, and of the years, the sequences of good and bad harvests in nature

'The North Sketch Sequence', 2014; Photograph: Sylvain Deleu

and in life, as well as the time of making, are all made visible for us. Van der Beugel comments, 'It is almost like it is a mantra, a mantra upon the idea that to extract meaning from anything, you need to employ effort and time.'

Van der Beugel's most famous project, however, was his next, 'The North Sketch Sequence', installed in Chatsworth House, the seat of the Duke of Devonshire, in 2014. Wall-sized panels of clay are embedded with a pattern of 6,000 clay wedges creating unique portraits of the Devonshire family, based upon their DNA. These bold and impressive works are instantly accessible as a concept but also wonderfully subtle in the myriad variations of texture and form of the wedges, each hand-formed. Van der Beugel explains: 'I have always been fascinated by the challenge of articulating the human condition and I feel science is the best way of understanding ourselves. So, when I did the Chatsworth project, there was a eureka moment, when these interests just aligned beautifully. I knew instantly that I couldn't really go back to making vessels. A pot just can't contain or hold those ambitions.'

The project led to a residency at The Wellcome Sanger Institute, a renowned genome-sequencing centre near Cambridge, and in 2019 van der Beugel completed a similar commission for the Dutch royal family, 'The DNA Room at Huis ten Bosch'. Van der Beugel is clear that he does not see his work as an illustration of science, but more a development through another medium and discipline of scientific ideas. 'I have worked with a Dutch professor called Robert Zwijnenberg at the University of Leiden,' he explains, 'and he and I have discussed at length the idea of artists being dazzled by science and using all these beautiful scientific techniques but not really bringing anything additional to the debate about how we use these technologies, what that says about ourselves, and the impact upon society – all these questions that are fundamental. I am trying to create an arena for these debates to happen.' That

'The North Sketch Sequence', 2014, detail; Photograph: Sylvain Deleu

is partly why scale is so important to him: 'Visual wonder is really important in art and that is why architectural spaces work for me because you can create literally a physical arena.'

In 2016, van der Beugel moved on to explore epidemiology, creating "Pathways of Patients" in collaboration with the Epidemiology Cancer Statistics Group based at York University. This moving work graphically represents the differing pathways for patients suffering from different blood cancers, using the rusting of iron rebar, sometimes referred to as 'concrete cancer', to create wriggly red lines through a concrete bed. As van der Beugel explains, 'Occurrences of blood cancers are not linked to the sociodemographic index (i.e. no one is more or less likely to get blood cancers), yet surviving and managing the disease successfully is linked to sociodemographics. 'Pathways of Patients' highlights this disparity and injustice in a unique way using concrete and rust. The length of the pathways denotes the length of life after diagnosis. In more affluent areas or groups the pathway continues and in poorer groups the pathway stops. The rust is evocative

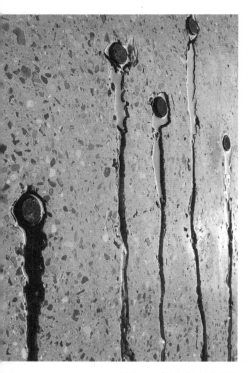

'Pathways of Patients', detail, 2016;
Photograph: Jacob van der Beugel

of blood and iron. The concrete becomes almost an urban biological tissue.' As well as a new kind of data, the project also introduced van der Beugel to concrete. He says, 'I used to think that fired clay and concrete were incredibly similar materials, both in their capacity to endure and in their ability to freeze gestures. But for me ceramic is most beautiful and most poignant when it is unglazed and textural and earthy, and you have really captured that connection with rock and clay as well as that interesting dialogue with man's input. With concrete I really use it to suggest that there is something going on beyond the surface. I skim off the layers to reveal what lies underneath.' Although he is conscious of concrete's environmental cost, he says, 'I like the fact that it is a common material and so under-appreciated. It is beautiful, because it is all these accumulations and aggregations of different stones and different sands brought together.' It is also a democratic material, used across all social environments, just as blood cancers afflict people equally across all socio-economic sectors.

Most recently van der Beugel has been working with self-healing concrete, an invention of Dr Henk Jonkers, in Delft, where bacteria introduced into the mix, once activated by water, can heal microscopic cracks in the concrete by creating calcite, a limestone. The idea that this might prove a more sustainable material has fed into his solo show, 'A Mutating Story', on view at the Dutch museum, Beelden aan Zee in The Hague. Here he uses the metaphor of 'self-healing concrete' to urge the audience to think about a future with enhanced human capabilities for self-healing at a cellular level. He is exploring similar ideas in an installation for The Lawrence J. Ellison Institute for Transformative Medicine in Los Angeles.

The idea of how we might endure engrosses van der Beugel – both how memory and legacy perpetuate the unique impact of individuals on the world, but also how, in the future, we might find novel ways to perpetuate our identities, our values and our ideas. In 2019, he completed a residency at The Wallace Collection in London, in honour of the 200th anniversary of its founder, Sir Richard Wallace. Now he is pondering the idea of using synthetic DNA to encode everything it is possible to know about a person, or even our cultural ideas about preservation, and embedding that in an artwork. What is certainly the case is that van der Beugel, far from being limited by his materials or his discipline, has made this 'mutating' practice yield in one after another arena of human thought.

'A Mutating Story' 2020;
Photograph: Gerrit Schreurs

READ
THE (CARBON)
LABEL

By translating carbon emission data into clear labelling on everyday products, a pioneering new wave of companies is aiming to cut global emissions by changing our habits for the better.

WORDS Ben Olsen
PHOTOGRAPHY Matt Palmer
ILLUSTRATION Blandine Pannequin
CARBON STATEMENTS Carbon Calories

'We need a paradigm shift: as informed global citizens we need to lead our global transformation behaviourally.'

The need for climate action is more pressing than ever. Against a backdrop of wildfires, coral bleaching and record recession of Greenland's ice sheet, time is short for world leaders to honour their promises to 2015's Paris Agreement, whose goal to limit future increases in global average temperature to just 1.5°C appears increasingly optimistic. The catastrophic potential of a rise greater than this figure – as documented in the Intergovernmental Panel on Climate Change's devastating 2018 report – means reducing our carbon emissions has become a necessity upon which our future depends.

Alexander Frantzen, the founder of New York-based Carbon Calories, doesn't intend to wait for state intervention. 'Nearly every country in the world made commitments to the Paris Agreement, but these remain empty until you put through legislation. We need a paradigm shift: as informed global citizens, we need to lead our global transformation behaviourally.' His team aims to catalyse and support the public's endeavour to reduce the carbon footprint of their lifestyles, through carbon accounting – the measuring and reporting of greenhouse gas emissions – and crystal-clear product-level reporting and labelling. By helping us understand the impact of our consumption habits, Frantzen hopes to empower us to make informed decisions about our actions that affect humanity and our planet.

Carbon Calories has created the world's first standardised, consumer-centric product Carbon Statements – easy-to-compare reports that illustrate the carbon footprint of everyday items, whether that's an orange, an iPhone or a cup of coffee. The term 'carbon' is often used to refer to all greenhouse gases. By analysing the carbon emissions – measured in CO2e, which stands for Carbon dioxide equivalent – at each stage of production and consumption, as well as factoring in scenarios for the potential number of uses, a Carbon Statement reports the total carbon emissions for a particular product. Take, for example, a T-shirt. Using publicly available data, Frantzen has created a Carbon Statement that shows the possible emissions in two very different scenarios. For a T-shirt made using conventionally grown cotton, worn 10 times and washed and machine dried using non-renewable energy, the carbon emissions are 560g per use. Yet if that T-shirt is made from zero-till cotton (where crops are grown without disturbing the soil through tillage), worn 50 times, washed using a machine fuelled by renewable energy and then hang-dried, that figure drops to just 70g.

To help us put these figures in context, another key tenet of Carbon Calories' work is the calculation of a Daily Carbon Quota (DCQ) for every human on the planet. The DCQ is arrived at by dividing this year's global greenhouse gas emissions budget by the total global population. This year the DCQ is 16,668g CO2e per day per person. With this in mind it is hoped that easy comparison of products and understanding the decisions that impact the carbon footprint of a product – in this instance, cotton type or drying method – will help us adjust our lifestyle for the better.

'Our statements work in a similar way to nutritional information labels,' says Frantzen, who created the website WikiCarbon as an open-source repository for the underlying inputs used in many of the Carbon Statements. 'People use nutrition labels to form a tacit knowledge – everyone knows a bag of chips will probably score highly for sodium or saturated fats. We need to formulate that same understanding for all lifestyle carbon emissions.'

According to Frantzen, the difficulty lies in how to communicate such complex information, illustrating his point using the example of red meat – a product often portrayed in a negative light. 'Objectively speaking, red meat isn't the problem – it's the way we produce and consume it,' he says. 'Utilising rotational grazing, for example, can reduce emissions and support soil carbon sequestration, while feeding cows kelp or algae supplements can significantly reduce methane during digestion. Eating this type of meat, and less of it, will mitigate deforestation and emissions.' Carbon Statements can help elucidate such factors. They increase our understanding of the different influences over a product's lifecycle and will therefore enable us to make more informed choices about our purchases, offering us the chance to choose the meat, for example, with the lowest possible carbon footprint.

Carbon accounting is not a new concept – product lifecycle assessments for environmental impact auditing were first developed in the 1960s. Decades later, corporate interest in measuring carbon output increased after the 2011 release of the Greenhouse Gas Protocol: a landmark set of standards and tools, released by the World Resources Institute and World Business Council for Sustainable Development, designed to consolidate the myriad different approaches to carbon accounting at the time. However, without government regulation there was, and is, still little incentive for companies to report their findings, preventing labelling from reaching supermarket shelves.

Labelling is only possible with consistent carbon accounting. Frantzen's start-up, which works with companies to prepare Carbon Statements for their products, is part of an ecosystem of organisations aiming to drive change in this area. The Carbon Trust's certification scheme is one of the largest, helping organisations demonstrate success in cutting their carbon footprint, while other pioneers, including CoolFarmTool, the Sustainability Consortium and Mondra, are improving visibility of carbon emissions across various sectors.

What's changed since 2011 is increased consumer demand. A recent Kearney report showed 78 per cent of consumers believed that companies should be doing more to help them make decisions that improve environmental outcomes, while in another survey – commissioned by the Carbon Trust – two-thirds of respondents supported carbon labelling on products. Upon its release, Hugh Jones, the Carbon Trust's managing director, said: 'Companies have much to gain by quantifying the carbon footprints of their products and services. Passing this information on to increasingly well-informed and climate-conscious consumers can enhance a company's reputation – and market share.'

This year has seen a turning point, with firms including Unilever, Oatly, Quorn and BASF committing to adding carbon footprint labelling to their products, while many more have begun to disclose information about the carbon emissions released along their supply chain for the first time. However, carbon accounting is expensive, with consultants costing vast sums, and supply chains can be incredibly nuanced as well as opaque. Previous attempts at implementing carbon footprint labelling have faltered, too, with Tesco introducing a scheme in 2007, which was dropped within five years because of its complexity.

This time around, a strong sense of urgency is driving organisations such as Carbon Calories to overcome these hurdles. 'Our efforts this decade will determine whether the 1.5°C cap is possible,' says Frantzen. 'We need to mitigate human-caused carbon emissions by half in this time frame, otherwise the planet will unavoidably warm by 2°C or more.'

Until carbon accounting is carried out by every company at every stage of production along the supply chain, there will always be a degree of approximation in carbon footprint labelling. But as the growing number of companies disclosing data leads to greater transparency, it's likely far more of us will take this message on board and demand change from the ground up.

CARBON STATEMENT COMPARISON

COFFEE AT HOME AUTOMATIC MACHINE

CARBON EMISSIONS PER USE (CO₂e*)	102 g
PRODUCTION STAGES	**39 g**
Agrochemicals production	26 g
Cultivation on plantation	6 g
Pre-processing	1 g
Milling, packaging and transport	3 g
Roasting and distribution	3 g
CONSUMPTION STAGES	**63 g**
Grinding and purchase	2 g
Preparation	60 g
End-of-life disposal	1 g
DAILY CARBON QUOTA**	**0.6%**

COFFEE AT HOME FRENCH PRESS

CARBON EMISSIONS PER USE (CO₂e*)	52 g
PRODUCTION STAGES	**39 g**
Agrochemicals production	26 g
Cultivation on plantation	6 g
Pre-processing	1 g
Milling, packaging and transport	3 g
Roasting and distribution	3 g
CONSUMPTION STAGES	**13 g**
Grinding and purchase	2 g
Preparation	10 g
End-of-life disposal	1 g
DAILY CARBON QUOTA**	**0.3%**

Gentle, soothing and undemanding tends to characterise the cooking at this time of year. As the nights draw in, meals need to sustain, warm and nourish. Stockpots are left to simmer, the season's earthy root vegetables surrendering their bite to soups and stews; and the oven resumes its role at the heart of the kitchen. Orchard fruits and hedgerow berries are baked into puddings, and casseroles and deep pie dishes arrive at the table. These are the sorts of recipe we're sharing in this issue.

We're also shining a spotlight on the cauliflower. Mild and unassuming, the creamy quality of the cloud-like curds is often overlooked in favour of broccoli and its other punchier relatives. Happily chefs and food writers have set out to shake up this humble vegetable's image and prove how flavoursome and versatile it can be. We've taken up the mantle too.

RECIPES Gaven Fuller and Dominique Park
PHOTOGRAPHY Lizzie Mayson
FOOD AND PROP STYLING Frankie Unsworth

Cauliflower and spiced toasted grains salad
with lemon, pistachio and spiced fruit

SERVES 4-6 AS A SIDE

135g buckwheat groats
135g bulgar wheat
500g cauliflower florets
    (about 1 medium cauliflower),
    finely chopped
65ml sunflower oil
10g ras el hanout
1 tbsp water
1 tbsp apple cider vinegar
40g currants
55g pomegranate seeds
40g pistachios
5g flat-leaf parsley,
    roughly chopped
5g coriander,
    roughly chopped
10g mint,
    roughly chopped
3 tbsp lemon juice
sea salt and black pepper

METHOD

Preheat your oven to 180ºC fan.

Cook the buckwheat and bulgar wheat in two separate pans of boiling water until they are just under done – they need to retain a slight bite. Drain well.

Place the cauliflower, buckwheat, bulgar wheat, sunflower oil, ras el hanout and some salt and pepper in a large bowl and toss to combine. Divide the mixture between two baking trays and roast for 15–20 minutes, until the grains are golden and puffed and the cauliflower is cooked through and golden brown. Remove from the oven and set aside to cool.

Meanwhile, in a small pan, heat the water and cider vinegar until one or two bubbles start to form on the surface then pour this over the currants and leave to stand for 10 minutes, allowing the currants to swell and absorb some of the liquid. Drain and dry the currants.

Place the cauliflower and toasted grains in a mixing bowl and add all the remaining ingredients, including the soaked currants. Toss to combine, then taste and check the seasoning, adding more salt and pepper if necessary. Transfer to a serving bowl.

Whole roast cauliflower
with a mustard, blue cheese and sage topping

**SERVES 4 AS A MAIN
OR 6 AS A SIDE**

1 tsp wholegrain mustard
½ tsp Dijon mustard
2 tsp olive oil, plus a little
    extra for greasing
1 garlic clove,
    finely grated
½ tsp ground turmeric
pinch of fennel seeds
1 large cauliflower
unsalted butter,
    melted, for basting
sea salt and
    black pepper

FOR THE TOPPING

1 tsp chopped sage
2 tsp fresh breadcrumbs
2 tsp rolled oats
40g blue cheese, grated
    (we'd go for Stichelton
    or Bledington Blue)

METHOD

Preheat your oven to 170ºC fan.

In a bowl, mix both mustards with the oil, garlic, turmeric, fennel seeds and a pinch of salt and pepper.

Cut a piece of foil, season it with salt, pepper and a splash of olive oil and place the cauliflower on top. Wrap the foil around the edges so that it comes halfway up the sides of the cauliflower and place on a small baking tray.

Massage the mustard mixture all over the florets and place in the oven (at the same time as your roast chicken, if using the chicken juices for basting – see note). Roast for around 50 minutes, basting liberally every 20 minutes with the roast chicken juices or with melted butter.

Meanwhile in a bowl, mix all the topping ingredients with a pinch of freshly cracked black pepper.

Once tender, remove the cauliflower from the oven, cover with the topping mixture and place it back in the oven for 8 minutes, or until the topping is golden and toasted. Serve straight away.

For meat eaters, this recipe works brilliantly if you're roasting a chicken directly on a shelf as you can sit the cauliflower on the shelf beneath and allow the juices to baste and infuse it with flavour. But it's also an ideal main course for vegetarians – just basted with butter instead – and served with a selection of steamed greens.

Roast cauliflower risotto
with toasted hazelnuts

SERVES 4

200g cauliflower,
    cut into bite-sized
    pieces
drizzle of olive oil
handful of hazelnuts
25g butter
½ medium onion,
    finely chopped
1 garlic clove,
    finely chopped
250g carnaroli rice
75ml white wine
300ml hot
    vegetable stock
80g Parmesan, grated
1 tsp chopped parsley
1 tsp chopped thyme
sea salt
    and black pepper

FOR THE
CAULIFLOWER PURÉE

1 medium onion,
    sliced
25g unsalted butter
225g cauliflower,
    broken down
    into florets
1 garlic clove,
    finely chopped
1 tsp lemon juice
75ml milk

METHOD

Start by making the cauliflower purée. Put the onion, butter and cauliflower into a heavy-bottomed pan over a medium heat and cook until the onion starts to turn soft and golden. Add the rest of the ingredients, seasoning with salt and pepper, bring to a simmer and cook until the cauliflower is soft in the centre, then blend and pass through a fine sieve.

Preheat the oven to 180ºC fan. Put the cauliflower into a roasting tin, drizzle with oil and toss with salt and pepper. Roast in the oven for 20–25 minutes, until tender and golden brown.

Turn the oven down to 170ºC fan, place the hazelnuts in a small baking tin and toast them in the oven for 5–7 minutes, keeping a close eye on them to check they don't catch and burn. Remove and roughly chop.

Meanwhile, melt the butter and a drizzle of oil in a large heavy-bottomed pan over a low–medium heat and add the onion and garlic. Leave the onion to sweat without allowing it to colour. Add the rice and slowly sweat for 5 minutes, stirring all the time.

Pour in the white wine and leave it to cook until all the liquid has gone, then add the hot stock a ladle at a time, stirring constantly. Repeat until all the stock has been used up – the rice should still have a little bite to it but not be crunchy. Taste and season.

Stir in the cauliflower purée and Parmesan, then add the roasted cauliflower and leave to cook for a couple of minutes. Finally, stir in the herbs. Divide between bowls and serve with the toasted hazelnuts scattered over the top.

This risotto has a wonderful combination of textures: the rice base is velvety and creamy thanks to the cauliflower purée; there is a soft bite from the roasted cauliflower; and the toasted hazelnuts add crunch.

Winter greens with ricotta and linguine

SERVES 4

100g Brussels sprouts,
   trimmed and finely
   sliced or shaved
100g curly kale,
   tough stems removed
300g linguine, or pasta
   shape of your choice
200–250g ricotta,
   depending on how
   thick you'd like it
handful of walnuts
sea salt
   and black pepper

FOR THE
CAVOLO NERO PESTO

250g cavolo nero,
roughly chopped
120g pumpkin seeds
2 garlic cloves,
   peeled and halved
350ml olive oil

METHOD

Start by making the pesto. In a medium bowl mix all the ingredients together with some salt and pepper and leave to stand for 10 minutes. Place in a blender and blend until it is a coarse paste (do not blend until smooth). Taste to check the seasoning.

Preheat your oven to 170ºC fan. Place the walnuts in a small baking tray and once the oven is hot, toast them for 3–4 minutes, keeping a close eye on them to make sure they don't catch and burn. Remove from the tray and roughly chop.

Bring one large and one small pan of salted water to the boil. Blanch the sprouts in the small pan for 30 seconds, then remove with a slotted spoon and blanch the kale leaves in the same way. Drain well, then roughly chop the kale.

In the large pan, cook the pasta until al dente (the timing will depend on your choice of shape). Strain, reserving a little of the cooking water, then return the pasta and reserved water to the pan and add the sprouts, kale and a good spoonful of the pesto. Stir, then add ricotta until you have reached your desired consistency. Season with salt and pepper, then serve in bowls topped with the toasted walnuts.

Pesto is such a useful thing to make in batches as it means you have the start of a meal ready in your freezer or fridge. This recipe makes a lot more pesto than you need, so either store the leftovers in a jar in the fridge, covered with a thin layer of oil for up to a week, or freeze it in ice-cube trays and defrost as needed.

Fennel and pear salad

SERVES 3–4 AS A SIDE

1 lemon
250g fennel
    (about 1 large head),
    trimmed and cut into
    2–3mm slices
100g peppery leaves,
    such as chicory,
    radicchio, watercress
½ firm pear
1 tbsp olive oil
sea salt
    and black pepper

TO SERVE (OPTIONAL)
around 80g crumbly
    sheep's cheese
    or feta-style cheese

METHOD

Squeeze the juice from half the lemon into a bowl of water and add the fennel – this will prevent the fennel from browning and retain its crispy texture.

When you're ready to serve, peel and slice the pear. Place the greens in a serving bowl or platter, drain the fennel and arrange it on top, along with the pear. Squeeze over the juice of the remaining lemon half, and add the olive oil and salt and pepper to taste. Toss well.

To serve, sprinkle over some crumbled sheep's cheese, if using. Serve immediately.

Turmeric seed porridge
with berries and kefir

SERVES 2

40g buckwheat groats
20g quinoa
15g chia seeds
2 tsp linseed
¼ tsp sea salt
½ tsp ground turmeric
splash of milk
    of your choice

TO SERVE

kefir or plain yoghurt
Manuka honey or raw
    honey with the comb
handful of seasonal
    berries or goji berries

METHOD

Put the buckwheat groats, quinoa, chia seeds and linseed into a bowl with 250ml water and leave to soak overnight.

The next day, drain the seeds and place in a small pan with 200ml fresh water, the salt and turmeric. Gently bring up to a boil and leave to simmer for 15 minutes, or until the buckwheat and quinoa are soft. At this stage, if you feel it's too thick for your taste, you can add a splash of milk to loosen the porridge.

Divide between two bowls and serve topped with a dollop of kefir or yoghurt, a drizzle of honey (and some of the comb, if using) and the berries.

Spiced plum and berry relish

MAKES 1.8-2KG

300g cooking apples, peeled, cored and chopped
260g plums, peeled, stoned and chopped
1 small red onion, finely diced
1 medium garlic clove
2 tsp grated ginger

small pinch of dried chilli flakes
1 tsp lemon juice
3 tbsp water
150g blackberries, hulled
170g granulated sugar
5 tbsp red wine vinegar

METHOD

Put the apples, plums, red onion, garlic, ginger, chilli, lemon juice and water into a preserving pan. Bring to a gentle boil and then leave to simmer until the plums and apples have broken down and are soft and pulpy – this should take 10–15 minutes. Add the blackberries and cook for another 5–10 minutes, until they soften.

Add the sugar and vinegar, stirring until dissolved. Bring to a simmer (with the lid off because you want to reduce the mixture to a jam consistency) and bubble for a further 4–6 minutes, until thick and glossy. Taste the relish to make sure it is not too vinegary – it should have a sweet but sour flavour. If needed, add a touch more sugar. Pour into sterilised jars (see note). Store in a cool place and use within 12 months. Once opened, store in the fridge and use within two weeks.

This recipe makes quite a substantial quantity but because the relish keeps for so long, it's a great way to preserve these fruits. You can transfer the finished relish into different sizes of sterilised jars (see below) and offer them as gifts at Christmastime or throughout the year.

To sterilise jars for preserves, heat your oven to 120ºC fan. Wash the jars in hot, soapy water, then rinse them well. Place the jars on a baking sheet and put them into the oven to dry. If you are using Kilner jars, you will need to remove the rubber seals and boil them, as the oven heat damages them.

Lemongrass poached plums
with toasted almonds

SERVES 4-6

1.5 litres water
3 lemongrass teabags
120g caster sugar
grated zest and juice
    of 1 large lemon
650g plums,
    halved and stoned

TO SERVE
flaked almonds
coconut or
    ginger ice cream
a few mint leaves

METHOD

Place the water in a medium pan with the teabags, sugar, lemon zest and juice and bring to a slow simmer until the sugar dissolves.

Add the plums, then bring the poaching liquid back to a gentle simmer and poach the plums for 5–10 minutes or until the plums are tender – the timing will depend on their ripeness.

If you have time, leave the plums submerged in the liquid for a couple of days to infuse.

Toast the almonds in an oven preheated to 170ºC fan for 3–5 minutes, keeping a close eye on them to check they don't catch and burn.

Serve the plums warm or at room temperature with ice cream, a drizzle of the poaching syrup and topped with the toasted almonds.

ROOTS ENTWINED

WORDS Fiona McCarthy
PHOTOGRAPHY Sarah Weal

Over the past few years, there has been a marked shift away from mechanised and digital lifestyles, towards embracing a more natural way of living. But for artisans such as Jenny Crisp, engaging with nature has been both the impetus and the root of her profession for over 35 years. As a willow grower and a basketmaker, that connection and attunement to her surroundings is inherent in her craft. Here, she reflects on a profession that is being rediscovered and appreciated by a new generation of makers, a passion and now a business she shares with her daughter, and why sitting down to embrace the slow, rhythmic process of weaving is when she is at her happiest.

'A basket definitely reflects its maker,' says Jenny Crisp, the Herefordshire-based willow grower and weaver whose elegant, refined pieces have been bought by royalty, used in award-winning films such as *Gladiator*, and held in the permanent collections of venerated institutions such as the V&A and the Crafts Council. 'Even though a basket can be made in the same material, possibly even in the same design, I can often tell who has made it because the maker's attitude and connection to the willow defines the end result.'

Since starting to make baskets 35 years ago, Jenny's distinctive hand can be seen in the tight, neat rigour she imbues into the clean-lined modernity of her pieces, from trivets and fruit bowls to gathering baskets and open-weave lampshades. 'If you work for speed [to fulfil orders], rather than quality, the outcome looks rough,' she says. 'I won't do that.'

Instead, she relishes bringing ancient techniques to life, looking to the ways willow has been used over the centuries, through old paintings or examples in museums, as inspiration for her sophisticated but subtle silhouettes, and the integration of interesting weaves in her pieces.

Indeed, as Jenny writes in her book *Willow: Traditional Craft for Modern Living*, her guide to growing, harvesting and making, her willow-weaving techniques are not new. Grasses have

long been woven into shoes, cloaks or carpets, and branches of small trees crafted into boxes, boats or houses. Yet, unlike the industrialisation of textile weaving or mass-casting of ceramic pots, any changes in basketmaking owe nothing to modern developments but to the mind and movement of the basketmaker.

In this, Jenny is as much artist as artisan. Her ambition to make 'the Rolls-Royce of baskets,' she says, has taken 'time and practice'.

'I have always wanted people to take my work seriously,' she says, reflecting back to a time when she first started making and her craft was seen as somehow romantic but less valuable than trades such as bricklaying or gate-making. 'I wanted to say to the world, "Yes, it looks like a wonderful way to live, but let's get real – to make this a real job, to pay the mortgage, you have to really know the technique and the material".'

Originally trained in woven textiles, graduating with a bachelor's degree with honours from the West Surrey College of Art and Design in 1985, Jenny found her true calling while researching the use of willow in basketmaking for her final thesis. 'Not because I was particularly interested in it,' she laughs, 'but because there seemed to be some connection between the two, especially in terms of strength and structure, which as a textile weaver interested me the most.'

'A basket reflects
its maker.'

It led to a year's apprenticeship, sponsored by the Crafts Council, and four further years working with the renowned Somerset-based basketmaker David Drew. 'I was intrigued by David and his wife Judy's way of life – they were almost self-sufficient, growing their own food and willow. It really impressed me,' Jenny remembers. 'When I met David, he was the only independent basketmaker growing his own material. After the arrival of imported goods in the 1950s and 60s, there was a massive and quick decline in willow growing and basketmaking,' she explains. By the time David came to basketmaking, only one type of willow, Black Maul, was being commercially grown. 'It was rather like weaving all of your different types of clothes out of one type of yarn,' she says.

Jenny's desire to grow her own willow, not only inspired by David, also came about

because, 'I loved both the symbiosis of growing an indigenous material to make an object and the outdoor nature of the work,' she enthuses. Black Maul also didn't suit the relatively unused making techniques she was keen to develop in her work. 'Growing my own willow gave me a wider palette – not only of colour but construction, scale, build and technique,' she says.

She grows mostly varieties of *Salix purpurea* (purple willow, named for its colourful catkins), *Salix viminalis* (osier willow, known for being strong, neat and bendy) and *Salix triandra* (almond-leaved willow), chosen for how good they feel in the hand and the lovely patina they bring to her work. 'You need an elegant willow to make an elegant piece; you need robust willow to make a strong piece,' she continues. She trusts her colour palette to Mother Nature –

'sometimes, if you put a certain colour next to another, a very grey willow might suddenly look blue. I could never make that happen with my textile patterns at college, but I can do that with the willow,' explains Jenny.

Today, there has been a renaissance in both willow growing, with companies like Somerset-based Musgrove Willows reintroducing old varieties grown by their founding grandfather in the 1920s, and basketmaking. Jenny has also seen a huge change in demographic at the workshops she holds regularly (not during Covid-19 times). Where once it might have just been women aged between 40 and 60 in her classes, 'in the last five years, I've had more young people coming along, totally committed to making baskets for a living. It's fantastic,' she beams.

One of those young makers has been her own daughter Issy Wilkes, a theatre and festival stage designer, with whom Jenny recently joined forces to create a new business, Willow with Roots. 'I never expected Issy to be a basketmaker,' Jenny admits. 'To be honest, I wanted her to have an easier way of earning a living. Basketmaking involves long, long hours and hard graft, working repetitively to understand how to respond to the material.'

'Growing my own willow gave me a wider palette – not only of colour but construction, scale, and technique. '

It's no surprise, however, that Issy's understanding of willow-weaving, learnt by osmosis while making her own little baskets by her mother's side as a child, had already crept into her own work creating large willow sculptures for festivals and theatre. But it was a commission for a collection of dramatic gourd-shaped wicker pendant shades for Netherwood Estate's Michelin-starred restaurant, Pensons, in Herefordshire, which opened in January 2019, that really sealed the collaboration.

'We thought it would be good for her to join me so she could learn how to use more controlled techniques – but then we found we really enjoyed working together and our creativity blossomed as a team,' says Jenny. 'Where I tend to be rather conservative in my consideration of design, perhaps restricted by the material and technique I know so well,' she admits, Issy's 'big sky' thinking 'challenges those boundaries of scale and combination of different materials.' Together, they have since produced a nine-metre-high wicker giant for the Boomtown Festival near Winchester, willow fairy sculptures for St Fagans National Museum of History in Cardiff, and willow fencing for a primary school in Worcestershire.

They also craft the chicest bulbous garden pods in ornate shades of Whissender, Black Maul and Brittany Green willow – designed originally as a series of sculptures for Jardin Blanc, Raymond Blanc's pop-up garden restaurant and bar at Chelsea Flower Show in 2019 – and ingenious flat-packed teepees. 'Sleepy Daisy' lampshades – in tones of buff, green and white willow, so called by Issy's daughter young Orla for the way the repeating loops of willow echo the way a daisy closes up at night – encourage lively shadow play across a room.

Yet, despite three decades of experience and world regard for her basketmaking prowess, Jenny's approach is still 'to take little steps at a time. What I enjoy is sitting down quietly on my own, in the workshop in my garden, trying to make the next thing as well as I can,' she says. 'It really suits me.'

Willow: Traditional Craft for Modern Living by Jenny Crisp is published by White Lion Publishing.

jennycrisp.co.uk
willowwithroots.co.uk

The ancient honey-based beverage is experiencing
a revival as modern microbreweries from South London
to Northumberland and New York discover the flavours
and natural probiotic benefits of a drink and a craft that
can also support local beekeepers.

MEAD

THE MODERN CRAFT BREWERIES
REDISCOVERING THE OLDEST ALCOHOLIC DRINK

WORDS Phoebe Hunt
PHOTOGRAPHY Martin Morrell

Honey mead is as old as the hills. The Egyptian Pharaohs treasured it, the Indian Maharajas commissioned poems about it, and the Ancient Greeks knew it as ambrosia, nectar of the gods. There is archaeological evidence that a fermented honey drink was made in China as early as 7000 BC, while references in millennia-old Vedic hymns talk too about mead's aphrodisiac power. In fact, the word 'honeymoon' is said to come from a pagan ritual of giving the newly married couple a month's supply of mead on their wedding night, its sweet intoxication a metaphor for young love.

At its most basic, mead is a sweet fermented alcoholic drink made from honey, water and naturally-occurring yeasts. When honey mixes with rainwater it becomes reactive, and in the presence of wild pollen it starts to ferment, so the first mead was probably discovered by accident in this way. In the English countryside, mead is entwined in our ancient traditions and history. It's the stuff of Vikings and King Arthur, Chaucer and Pliny the Elder – a forgotten elixir of days gone by. As wine and spirits became more accessible, however, mead's popularity waned in the twentieth century until it was almost forgotten about.

But the last few years have seen something of a revival in mead, as micro-breweries bring a modern approach to ancient methods and a small but growing community of craft mead makers now produce lightly sparkling, dry mead, that's not dissimilar to a prosecco or cider.

As London mead maker and entrepreneur Tom Gosnell points out, the drink has been left for decades to history enthusiasts and museum gift shops, sold in novelty flagons in places like Lindisfarne. Not so anymore. Now, Gosnell runs one of the UK's leading meaderies from his trendy Peckham warehouse, turning out more than 350,000 cans of lightly sparkling mead each year.

Gosnell is keen to stay away from too many historical associations. 'Mead has a great story, but this often obscures the fact that it's an amazing low-intervention, natural product made from nothing but honey, water and yeast. People think of traditional mead as quite strong, but ours is light at 4–5.5 per cent ABV and has subtle, refined flavours for the modern palate. It's a wonderful alternative to cider and is a good pairing for cheese. The fizziness was actually an accident during some experiments but it adds to the drinking experience and brings out the flavours, so we just stuck with it.'

English winemakers Mereworth Wines of Kent are also getting involved, producing a lightly carbonated mead 'spritz', a lighter twist on the sweet, syrupy traditional mead of yore. Owner William Boscawen launched 'Marourde' a few years ago. 'We were interested by the complexity and depth that mead can offer, so we used the craftsmanship of winemaking techniques to respond to modern palates.'

Companies like Gosnells, Mereworth and Irish-based Kinsale are appearing on the market fast, and mead makers have good reason to be optimistic. In the US, where trends like kombucha and craft beer were reliable forecasts for the UK drinks market, mead is one of the fastest-growing alcoholic drink sectors. The American Mead Makers Association has recorded more than 2000 per cent growth over the last decade, with a new meadery opening every three days on average.

While many mead makers sadly import most of their honey to keep costs down, there are meaderies that champion local beekeepers. Honey Spirits Co uses all local honey from the Peak District, and Wye Valley Meadery sources exclusively Welsh honey.

CUSTOMISE YOUR MEAD WITH HERBS AND FLOWERS

Flowers and herbs have natural properties to help successful fermentation, as well as adding extra flavour dimensions.

200g hawthorn and calendula flowers can be used as wild yeasts, instead of or combined with the blackberries.

3–4 olive leaves can be added for extra tannins.

A pinch of dried hibiscus flowers will give a rosé appearance and a slight tartness.

A few elderflower heads will add a floral perfume.

Combinations of festive spices, such as 1–2 cinnamon sticks, a teaspoonful of cloves and a star anise can balance a sweet mead nicely.

Northumberland Honey Co makes wildflower sparkling mead using honey from their 200 hives, following a champagne method of in-bottle fermentation to produce a crisp, sparkling mouthfeel. Sustainability is key for founders Suzie and Luke Hutchinson, who explain that each bottle purchased has allowed them to finance more hives and increase bee numbers, and that their process has no waste products.

'As beekeepers we are entirely focused on the welfare of our bees, providing them with the environment to make the best honey,' say Suzie and Luke. 'Mead brings out the subtle flavours and aromas in honey which are normally masked by its sweetness, so using good-quality wildflower honey makes a huge difference to the end product. We hope that as our mead grows in popularity we'll have the ability to shine a spotlight on the good work that sustainable beekeepers are doing, and as a whole support the beekeeping industry. This is especially important in the UK where there are currently only around 400 commercial beekeepers.'

Jonathan Chambers, who makes mead from his Clapham kitchen in London and is getting ready to launch a small business, believes the English sparkling wine market should be the target for mead makers. 'The continued success of companies like Nyetimber shows there's a demand for home-grown sparkling options, and mead has the potential to capitalise on this market and bring something new to the table.'

While there's a real science to making mead that's consistent enough to sell, there's no reason why you can't have a go at making it yourself. Penny Allen, who teaches the art of fermentation at Ballymaloe Cookery School near Cork in Ireland, encourages foraging for wild yeasts from blackberries or hedgerow flowers and letting them work their magic.

'In the past, if honey was stored in any kind of vessel and water got in, the honey would spontaneously begin to ferment as it already contains the wild yeasts needed for fermentation. Honey is always ready to ferment; you just need to help it along by making the right conditions for fermentation,' explains Allen.

Here, Allen shares a recipe for making your own mead using naturally-occurring wild yeasts and foraged flowers.

Homemade mead

Recipe by Penny Allen, Ballymaloe Cookery School

MAKES 4 LITRES

1.5 litres water,
    at room temperature,
    preferably filtered
800g raw local honey
    (about 3 jars,
    depending on
    their size)
200g wild blackberries
a handful of raisins
juice of 1 orange

YOU WILL ALSO NEED:

1 x 3-litre Kilner jar
    with a wide mouth
1 x 4-litre carboy,
    with an airlock filled
    with vodka

METHOD

1. The night before you're going to make your mead, you need to dechlorinate the water. Simply leave a jug of 1.5 litres of water out overnight, uncovered, and the chlorine will evaporate.

2. Sterilise the Kilner jar, then pour in the water and add 550g of the honey. Stir the honey and water together vigorously for at least 5 minutes.

3. Add the wild blackberries (or other edible wild fruit or flowers – see opposite).

4. Cover the top of the jar with a clean cloth secured with an elastic band (but leave the lid off). Leave the jar on a work surface somewhere warm where it won't get forgotten about – a warm kitchen is perfect.

5. Stir the honey water a few times daily (for as long as you can!), when you are passing by. The more you stir it, the more oxygen is introduced and the quicker the yeasts will become active. These yeasts are hungry microorganisms that will feed on the sugars in the honey, transforming them into alcohol.

6. After 3–5 days of stirring you should see fermentation happening – lots of bubbles will start to appear. Carbon dioxide is the by-product of alcohol fermentation and bubbles are the best indicator that mead is on the way.

7. Once it is successfully fermenting, strain the blackberries, stir in the remaining honey (more food for the yeasts), add the raisins (for their tannins, which balance the sweetness) and orange juice. These will all encourage the correct, alcohol-creating yeasts.

8. Decant your lively mead into a 4-litre carboy, top up with water to the neck of the carboy and seal with a one-way airlock, filled with vodka, to keep it sterile. It's essential to use an airlock rather than just a cork, otherwise you risk the vessel exploding.

9. Leave the liquid to ferment for a further 3 weeks and taste it as often as you like – it's always interesting to see how the flavour transforms over time. It should be sweet, but not overly so, and mildly alcoholic.

10. When the mead is to your liking, decant it into sterilised bottles, carefully leaving the sediment behind, and making sure to completely fill the bottles so there is no air in there. The mead will last in the fridge for at least two months, but is best enjoyed in the first couple of weeks.

There is no recommended serving glass for mead. A sparkling mead would suit a champagne flute or coupe, but you could also serve it in an elegant tumbler as you might a cider.

TRAVEL
IS PRECIOUS

WORDS Alice B-B
ILLUSTRATION Blandine Pannequin

It had become too easy, too selfish, too gluttonous. The world had suddenly become so small, many of us whizzing around it willy-nilly without a thought for the consequences of our footprint, only seeking to sate our thirst for instant gratification. Something had to give...

But the brutal pause inflicted by Covid-19 doesn't mean an end to adventure. Quite the opposite. It means making your adventures count. Travel consciously. Explore your own country. Plan trips with conservation-led travel agents. Build in time to give back – not just financially. Stay in places with sustainability at their core. Consider boutique hotels where your tourist dollar is more likely to filter down to the surrounding food chain, rather than filling corporate pockets of chain hotels. Meet locals. Talk to strangers. Listen to their stories; hear their truth about issues affecting land, livelihood, nature and habitat. Find out if there's a local conservation project, NGO or charity that needs support or funding. Give your time. Make the effort. And if you can't help in the moment, share the tales on your return with others who can make a difference.

Covid-19 has forced us to take a step back. It feels savage. But it's also pulled back the curtain, given us time to look at ourselves and our actions. It has revealed a huge opportunity; to be less selfish, to understand that we're all connected. And while it's an incredibly hard time for many, pain is the agent of change. And significant change is what the planet is crying out for. Travel is precious; let's honour it. Here are three of my dream adventures with potential for huge positive impact.

ECUADOR

A journey deep into the Ecuadorian Amazon with activist Zoë Tryon, who lived for many months with the Achuar tribe. Starting with a 'toxitour' in the north; you visit the land that has been ravaged by oil extraction and the people affected by it. This is followed by a dramatic contrast – a deep insertion into the magical and pristine land in southern Ecuador, the sacred headland of the Amazon river, which is currently under threat of being sold to oil conglomerates by the government. 'People who've been on my trips often become ambassadors for this situation and feel moved to support and fundraise,' explains Zoë. 'It's such an intensely eye-opening experience that often successful and powerful people feel compelled to make changes closer to home, making decisions to live more sustainably, while some choose to restructure the way their businesses are run. They've seen first-hand how the way we live and the way we conduct business can have a direct effect on the Amazon and its people.'
www.zoetryon.com

ANGOLA

No one knows how big the herds of elephant are in Angola. They're undocumented, but the rumoured numbers are huge and need protecting. Henry Cookson, founder of Cookson Travel, and with two polar world records under his belt, will lead this intrepid adventure; exploring vast swathes of untouched Africa, accompanied by vets, scientists, researchers, conservationists while working with locals on the ground in desperate need of funding. Angola won't be opening up for mass tourism any time soon – so philanthropic trips such as this will be setting a precedent and shaping the future.
www.cooksonadventures.com

VAMIZI

It's the modern-day fairytale: could the mythical, prehistoric coelacanth fish – thought to be extinct until rediscovered in 1938 – exist off the coast of Mozambique, among the deep caves and reefs of Vamizi Island? Because if just one of this critically endangered species was to be found, it would change everything for this massively important, diverse ecosystem, currently under threat from illegal fishing, habitat decimation and oil and gas extraction infrastructure. Working with Oceans without Borders' marine biologist Tessa Hempson, this epic adventure includes diving in a submersible to explore the deep waters. And in the event of discovering the evolutionarily important coelacanth (believed to be the 66 million-year-old missing link between aquatic fish and land-based tetrapods), this would exponentially help to expand and strengthen marine protected areas in the northern Quirimbas archipelago.
www.andbeyond.com

CALL OF THE WILD

EXPLORING THE STRETCHES OF THE SCOTTISH HIGHLANDS THAT ARE
BEING REPLENISHED AND RETURNED TO WILDERNESS

WORDS Lisa Grainger
PHOTOGRAPHY Richard Gaston (landscapes), Alex Baxter (interiors)

Sometimes, if you're lucky, a sense of happiness washes over you, which makes you realise that you are precisely in the right place at the right time – and that there's nothing that could be added or taken away to make that moment more perfect. Right then, all you can do is hold on to the feeling for as long as you can: to capture it in your brain, like a precious nugget of golden pleasure that can be retrieved and re-polished when life feels a little grey.

As a travel writer, I'm lucky to have nuggets in my head that I've stashed from journeys around the world: from watching herds of wildebeest migrating across the Serengeti; sitting on a seabed, looking up at giant manta rays doing balletic backflips in the Coral Sea; skiing down Alpine slopes in the sunshine with snowflakes sparkling on my eyelashes; and, of course, from walking in Scotland.

Scotland is the one place to which I travel and always return with a nugget. Perhaps that's because, like so many other outliers who have landed on our island's northern shores, from Viking sailors to English aristocrats, now that I have felt the pull of its wild spaces, I'm addicted.

This is a country that has an abundance of natural highs to take in. Within some of the largest tracts of unpopulated countryside in Europe (just 5.5 million people in an area three-fifths the size of England) lie some of this island's most spectacular landscapes. Sand beaches that are as white as those in the Caribbean (if a little nippier). The largest national park in the UK (the Cairngorms) and all 10 of its highest mountains. Plus, perhaps most importantly – if, as I do, you find joy in imbibing oxygen-rich air while walking in nature – seven of Britain's largest forests in which to wander and lose yourself among trees and streams and sky. In other words, it's a pretty good place in which to accumulate happiness.

Like others before him, it was Scotland's natural beauty that first brought Anders Holch Povlsen to these shores. Having fished and walked its wildernesses as a boy, with his father, Troels, who founded the fashion empire Bestseller, when the Dane returned as an adult, he packed not only a rod but a chequebook to buy an estate of his own. Since 1996, he and his wife, Anne Storm Pederson, have invested in a further 12: in Sutherland, the Cairngorms and alongside Loch Ness, making them the official caretakers of 220,000 acres and the largest private landowners in Britain.

Unlike many other large landowners, however, the Povlsens are not interested in hunting. As the website of their company, Wildland, which marries conservation and tourism, puts it: 'This is an investment in hope. A chance to let nature heal, grow and thrive.' The couple

have spent tens of millions of pounds planting more than 4 million tree saplings in the Cairngorms, taking down hundreds of miles of fences, reducing vastly over-stocked deer populations and restoring thousands of acres of ancient bogs. Their aim, they say, is 'very simple: we wish to restore our parts of the Scottish Highlands to their former natural splendour'.

While many of us associate Scotland's landscapes as being wild and untouched, they are far from natural I learn as I drive through Glenfeshie estate with Thomas MacDonnell, the head of conservation at Wildland, which manages Povlsen's estates.

When the Romans arrived, MacDonnell explains, the Highlands and islands were covered in ancient forests – hence their name for it: Caledonia, or 'wooded heights'. The country, though, needed wood: to build ships, infrastructure and housing, and to fuel industrialisation. By the end of the Second World War, not only had most of those ancient Caledonian forests been destroyed in the name of progress, but any saplings that had sprouted had been browsed by deer, bred to feed the Victorian fashion for shooting.

It was the Earth Summit in 2000, says MacDonnell, that cemented Povlsen's belief that he should do something to replenish the landscape and restore the great forests of Caledonia. 'I think that – like a lot of people – he recognised that if

he was able to, he had a responsibility to protect the environment... When he was here, on Glenfeshie, and saw some of the original forests that remained – alongside the scars from 1798, when 10,000 trees that had been planted in the 1500s were chopped down – he knew what he had to do. And Wildland was born.'

There are lots of things that contribute to creating happiness. While forests and good mountain air often set the scene for magical moments, cosy interiors, delicious locally-sourced food and welcoming hosts certainly add an extra sparkle. Which is where Povlsen's wife, Anne, comes in.

With the help of her designer friend Ruth Kramer, who owns the Swiss hotel Brücke 49 in Vals, Anne has created spaces ranging from designer farmhouse hotels and luxurious rental homes to cool self-catering cottages that reflect not only her Danish roots but her clear love of Scottish fabrics, landscapes and crafts.

The unique aesthetic created by the pair is prevalent in all of the Wildland properties, whether it's a castle that has housed queens (Aldourie) or a simple cottage for two in the Highlands (Kyle House). Each is a space in which you can pull off your wellies and indulge in the best kind of basics: cake that's just been baked, whose homespun smell hits you the minute you walk through the door; a log fire and pine cones crackling in the hearth; a hot bath infused with organic bath oil.

Plus, fashion and design books to read; fine art and vases of sculptural wild flowers to admire; and a super-comfy Scandinavian bed to fall into as the stars come out over Britain's most unpolluted skies.

Like the rest of their properties, Killiehuntly, the elegant, early seventeenth-century Cairngorms farmhouse in which I stay on my first Wildland visit, is the embodiment of hygge, the Scandinavian concept of cosiness. The fact that the old four-bedroomed stone farmhouse is so earthy, simple and unostentatious is because, I discover, the Povlsens, like many Scandinavians, adhere to Jante Law, the cultural ethos that encourages people to live life in a thoughtful and modest way. It is why, when you walk into a room, every item is carefully considered. Simple Orkney chairs are draped in cosy sheepskin and the hall table is piled with Norwegian jumpers, in case you're cold. Weathered milk stools bear pared-back Scandi-style

lamps (should you want to read) and handblown glass decanters (in case you're thirsty). Even the delicious food, presented on earthy stoneware by Danish potter Kaspar Würtz, is prepared using ingredients sourced from nearby farms, a thoughtful attempt to support locals and to create jobs in the countryside. As MacDonnell puts it: 'What we're trying to do is not just protect trees and wildlife, but create jobs and a long-term, sustainable nature-based economy.'

Although the interiors are so cosy that it's tempting to spend all your time indoors, the thousands of acres of nature around these properties is the reason you go to them. Whether it's the forests of Glenfeshie, in which *Brave*, *Outlander* and *Mary Queen of Scots* were filmed, the Munros and wide beaches of Sutherland, or the loch that lies at the ends of the lawns at Aldourie Castle, at a Wildland property, it's pretty hard to resist the pull of nature outdoors.

Which is why, rather than lie swathed in soft Lithuanian linen sheets at Killiehuntly, I sprang up early one morning to head off alone up a forested hill. With nothing but nature and the peaks of the Cairngorms to distract me, I had hours in which to focus on the smells and sounds of this wild patch of stillness: the waves of morning mist rising off the black, peaty earth, the burbling of a fast-running brook beside my pine-needle-strewn path, the whoosh of the breeze through the trees around me and, above, ominous clouds storming across the moody skies.

On another morning, from Lundies House, in the very north of Scotland, I set off on an electric bicycle and spent the whole day out in the crisp, autumnal air: walking along the wide, creamy sands of Skinnet beach, whizzing effortlessly up heather-clad hills, picnicking beside a burn. And, most memorably, on one of those rare, perfectly blue summer's days in Scotland, I kayaked the length of a loch with a passionate young Wilderness Scotland guide, who shared his knowledge about eagles and

trout, and the Highland Clearances – and then hiked with me to a bothy in which Wildland staff had set up one of the most perfect lunches of my life. It was memorable not only because I was hungry (we all know the effect a growling stomach has on our appreciation for food), or because, above hills aglow with rust- and lavender-coloured heather, we had panoramic views of Ben Hope soaring into the heavens. Or that there was a log fire blazing and the tantalising smell of Cullen skink wafting from an iron pot above it. Rather, it was the attention that had been put into arranging this timeless tablescape, with its wonky pottery bowls of pickles, its squat vases sprouting flowering heather, and its wooden platters of Scottish pâtés and fish and breads and cheeses, all candlelit like a medieval Flemish still life. And it was the Scottish staff's palpable pride in their country – and the parts they are playing, with Wildland, in restoring their landscapes, their villages, their communities and culture – that was utterly intoxicating. There's nothing like meeting people who love what they do to make you fall in love too.

wildland.scot

WINTER PLANTING

OPPORTUNITIES FOR GROWING VEG

For effective plant growth you need water, warmth and light. Winter often means limited warmth and light, thus it is known as the 'dormant' season. Plants grow very little when temperatures are below 8°C but when temperatures creep above this, established crops, such as kale, spinach, rocket and leeks, will all put on small amounts of growth and generate more harvestable leaf, but which crops can be planted during the colder months to give us a head start on the spring growing season?

WORDS Jez Taylor – PHOTOGRAPHY Matthew Gorman

BIG, SEEDED AND HARDY

Broad beans are such a large seed they will willingly germinate in the cooler soils of late October to mid November. The inherent energy stored within the seed will allow the seedling to become a sturdy 20cm plant to overwinter; indeed if planted any earlier the plants can become a little too tall and susceptible to frost damage. It's wise to cover your crop with mesh or netting as the sprouting seeds are a favourite of crows and pigeons – not surprisingly, as the broad bean presents the most nutritious source of vegetable protein in our UK climate. Sowing at this time will give you a three-week head start on any harvestable yields to be gained from a March sowing, which means you'll be eating the beans by mid June. Being leguminous (nitrogen fixing), broad beans are also an essential part of maximising soil fertility in organic growing systems, and are a great late-planted 'cover crop' to protect the soil over winter. Make sure you use the frost-hardy variety Aquadulce Claudia.

GARLIC

I am often dismayed when I read in gardening books that you can plant garlic as late as March. If you want big bulbs (I'm not a fan of fiddly small bulbs) then you need to get the cloves in the ground by mid November, planting them in well-drained soil (they will rot if waterlogged). Garlic is relatively trouble free, with few pests, and is ready for harvest once fully bulbed up from late June. But if you plant sufficient, the smaller bulbs can be harvested early and used like a garlicky leek from early May, a welcome opportunity during the 'hungry gap'. If you do miss the ideal planting time then cloves can be planted into pots of compost at any time over winter and brought on indoors for planting out in March.

PERENNIAL VEGETABLES

Another way to get early harvests is from crops that already have an established root system. Rhubarb, sea kale, globe artichokes, asparagus, chives and Good King Henry (a type of perennial spinach) behave like herbaceous perennials and die back in the winter, but as spring temperatures climb they are quick to respond with rapid growth. They are best planted during the dormant season, November and February being the ideal months; avoid the depths of winter when soil can be too wet to dig, and before delicate shoots can be damaged as we move into the warmth of March.

It will take at least 2–3 years before you can rely on significant harvests from these perennials so

it is important to dig them in (and later mulch with) plenty of compost to ensure you maximise nutrient supply. For those perennials that can be divided (all of the above except asparagus), you could get a much faster start by taking a division from a friend rather than buying a disappointingly small plant by mail order. Offering to mulch the plant with a bag of compost will make a fair exchange for a chunk off the side. Many of the rhubarb plants I have planted over the years have come from divisions of my father's 30-year-old rhubarb patch.

EARLY SOWING

If you have a greenhouse or cloches, then you have the ability to warm up soil, creating great conditions to germinate large-seeded vegetables, such as peas, beetroot, spinach and radish. Late January or February sowings offer significant head starts on crops sown in March or April and slugs are often still hibernating during this period, which helps avoid the potential slug plague of a wet April or May.

THERE'S ALWAYS THE WINDOWSILL

If outdoor space is an issue you can try growing nutritious microleaves on a sunny windowsill. Peas, coriander, beetroot and rocket can give a crop within 2–3 weeks. It is possible to grow cress seedlings on layers of wet tissue, but I prefer to grow them in seed trays in at least 3cm of compost/soil. This allows the seedlings to grow a bit bigger and the larger water-holding capacity of the compost means that watering isn't required as regularly and there is less risk of them drying out. Low-cost LED grow bulbs have made successful microleaf-growing indoors feasible on even the shadiest of windowsills, allowing the fussier herbs like dill, fennel and basil to be grown as long as temperatures stay above 16°C.

OR BESIDE THE KITCHEN SINK

The simplest way to enhance the nutritional opportunities of seed is to germinate or 'sprout' them. Mung beans and green lentils can be sprouted in a Kilner jar: just add 50g of seeds to a 1-litre jar, fill the jar with water and leave to soak overnight, then drain and rinse the seeds every 12 hours.

By taking every opportunity to grow and consume seasonal vegetables, you are engaging with and supporting a more sustainable food culture, which is essential to how we can all prosper in the future.

**LATE OCTOBER
MID NOVEMBER**
Broad beans
Garlic

•

**NOVEMBER
OR FEBRUARY**
Rhubarb
Sea kale
Globe artichokes
Asparagus
Chives
Good King Henry

•

**LATE JANUARY
FEBRUARY**
Peas
Beetroot
Spinach
Radish

Jez Taylor has been managing the market garden at Daylesford farm since 2008. He grows over 500 varieties of fruit and vegetable organically as well as a range of cut flowers.

GARDEN CRAFTS

BLOCK PRINTING WITH POTATOES AND OTHER SEASONAL
ACTIVITIES INSPIRED BY THE OUTDOORS

I was a complete tomboy as a child and spent my days running around after my two elder brothers. We grew up on a farm and, come rain or shine, most of our days were spent outside.

Throughout the year, I would spend hours foraging in the woodland collecting treasures to take home at the end of the day. Our farm manager, Keith Howard, was an absolute hero of mine and I am sure that my love of nature came from him. Whether it was damsons or walnuts, cobnuts or pears, there was always something interesting he'd enjoy sharing with us.

My mother also taught me about the seasons and the changing colour of leaves, and every autumn we would scoop up great bundles of them for leaf rubbing. There's so much to learn about the different leaves you can find and it was always fun matching the leaves to trees when we got home. My children love doing the same and go out armed with baskets and often a magnifying glass to take a closer look. They like sticking them in scrapbooks with little arrows stating what they've found where. Leaf rubbing is a great activity for all ages – it makes wonderful instant art pieces and they can be turned into all sorts of things. It's very easy to do; you just put a single leaf on a clipboard or secure it on a piece of card with some tape, then put a piece of paper over the leaf. Children can then use whatever they like – pastels, crayons or colouring pencils – to rub over the leaf and reveal its beauty. My youngest likes using good old-fashioned crayons and the older ones enjoy experimenting with different things: chalk and oil pastels make great markings.

I love our vegetable patch and come the autumn, there's so much to harvest. Eating our own potatoes is a dream. There is something very satisfying about digging up your own potatoes and eating them the same day and growing them is easier than you think. Even if you don't have lots of space, pots make a great home for potato plants. My children like helping with the sowing and we grow all sorts of different varieties, from first and second earlies, through to maincrop and decide which we all like best for roasting, baking, boiling or mashing. Some of our favourites are: Pink Fir Apple, Ratte, Kestrel, Cara, King Edward and Desiree. With over 500 varieties to choose from, it's always fun to try new ones.

WORDS Leonora Bamford
PHOTOGRAPHY Martin Morrell

I have fond childhood memories of using old potatoes to print with on a rainy day; being able to turn them into personalised blocks to stamp was such fun. It is still one of my favourite activities to do with the children and they have taken it one step further and like to print on to material too. With only a few things needed from around the house, it couldn't be an easier craft and everyone has a different result. So why not take a trip down memory lane and turn your hand to leaf rubbing and block printing? I'll be doing the same.

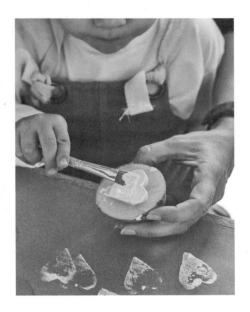

TO MAKE
block prints
from
potatoes

YOU WILL NEED:

medium to large potatoes
knife
cookie cutters
acrylic or fabric paint
paintbrush
paper or fabric

Using a sharp knife, cut the potato in half. Use a cookie cutter or knife to carve a design into the surface of the potato – I find simple shapes work best. If you're using a cookie cutter, press it into the potato – about 1cm in – and then cut around it with a knife (if you are letting your children cut their own, make sure you're watching carefully as the knife can easily slip).

Apply paint to the stamp using a paintbrush and then apply even pressure when pressing down on your desired surface.

A TABLE
FOR
AUTUMN

PHOTOGRAPHY
Martin Morrell

STYLING
Claudie Dubost
Frankie Unsworth

PREVIOUS SPREAD, clockwise from centre: Amwell red wine glass in smoke, available from Canvas Home; small Olive glass, Jack cutlery set, Marbled dinner plate, Marbled dessert plate, all available at Daylesford, various locations; table cloth, napkin, vase, bottles and candlesticks – all vintage

ABOVE, clockwise from centre: Amwell red wine glass in smoke, available from Canvas Home; Olive glass (small), Jack cutlery set, Marbled dinner plate, Marbled pasta plate, all available at Daylesford, various locations; table cloth, napkin, vase – all vintage

LEFT: Marbled dessert plate, Marbled pasta plate; vintage black bowl and napkin

FAR LEFT: Marbled curved jug; vintage table cloth and plate

A COMMAND
FROM NATURE

WORDS Satish Kumar
ILLUSTRATION Marc Majewski

The Covid-19 crisis has been a paradox. On the one hand, large numbers of people have suffered and many have experienced deep pain due to the loss of loved ones. On the other, millions have been offered an opportunity to slow down. They have used this time for spiritual retreat, for reflection, reading and renewal.

Many people have been described as being in 'quarantine'. When I looked up the etymology of the word I found that it referred to the period of 40 days that Jesus Christ spent fasting in the desert. Later the word became associated with the 40 days of Lent. Such periods of solitude are common in most religious traditions. Muslims have 40 days of Ramadan when they fast, pray and do some charitable work or community service. Buddhists and Jains have a similar period of spiritual retreat during the rainy season, when they stop travelling, suspend business activities and focus on forgiveness, fasting and the study of sacred texts. Jews have the Sabbath and a period of 40 days of reflection and spiritual transformation between Elul and Yom Kippur. These ancient traditions have

Satish Kumar is the Editor Emeritus of Resurgence
& Ecologist *and the author of* Elegant Simplicity.

a profound meaning in the minds and lives of people.

But in our age of materialism, the majority of people have forgotten the value of slow, simple and spiritual ways of life. The money machine never stops and most of us are on a 24/7 treadmill.

These activities of production and consumption are causing stress and strain to our natural environment. Our oceans are polluted with plastic waste, our fields are full of harmful chemicals, the rainforests are being cut down at an alarming rate, our atmosphere is saturated with greenhouse gases and enormous carbon emissions are causing climate change. This culture of needless consumption and wasteful production is not only damaging our natural environment, it is also causing untold misery to human life. The age of economy has turned into the age of anxiety, insecurity, loneliness and mental distress. The use of imagination and creativity is in decline.

In this age of materialism, nature and people have become a resource for the economy; they are used as a means to make profit. We need a paradigm shift. We need to shift our focus from economic growth to growth in wellbeing for people and planet. Nature is not simply an economic resource, it is the source of life. Everything born is nature – be it majestic mountains gracing the landscape, beautiful birds flying in the sky, lions living in jungles or humans dwelling in the cities. We are all nature, we are all members of one earth community and one earth family. Evolution teaches us that from the Big Bang to the present moment all life has shared the same origin and we have evolved together. As from one single apple seed we get a trunk, branches, leaves, blossoms and fruit, from one single point of the Big Bang we got this magnificent Tree of Life.

I believe the Covid-19 crisis came to us as a command from nature, ordering humanity to slow down and reduce its negative impact on the environment. This time we had to, and we did, listen to the voice of the earth. And the earth, too, found space to recover. A crisis is also an opportunity, and the crisis of the pandemic enabled many to seize an opportunity to manifest love,

generosity and humility. We witnessed marvellous manifestations of kindness and self-sacrifice around the world. Many people, particularly the young, came out of their confinement to help others who needed support. Mutual aid groups sprung up and volunteers offered their services with enthusiasm and passion. These were the heroes of the human spirit.

As in nature, everything passes, and this Covid-19 crisis too will pass. But are we going to go back to business as usual? Or will we learn to live in harmony with the natural world and in harmony with people of different races, religions, cultures and nationalities? Are we willing to find a balance between material values and spiritual values? If we can practise love, compassion, caring and crafts in abnormal times then why not also in normal times?

These are questions of paramount importance in the post-Covid period. Let us contemplate these questions personally and collectively. When we ask the right questions we will find the right answers.

Hushed is the buzz of the noisy world

Hushed is the buzz of the noisy world,
Gently each bird to its home is flitting,
The flags o'er the sun's bright path are furled,
Soon will each flower with the dew be pearled
As asleep it lies unwitting.

Spell-bound is the ever-whispering air,
For, gazing aloft where the stars are peeping
In this holy silence everywhere
Tired Nature speaks in a fervent prayer
To Him who protects her sleeping.

– George Gissing